DATE		

Small-Batch
Canning & Freezing
Cookbook

by Charlotte Turgeon

Illustrations by Lucian Lupinski

The Curtis Publishing Company
Indianapolis, Indiana

THE SATURDAY EVENING POST

Small-Batch Canning & Freezing Cookbook

Recipes that bring the summer garden to the winter table

The Saturday Evening Post
Small-Batch Canning & Freezing Cookbook
Jean White, Editor
Sandra Strother-Young, Art Director and Designer
Astrid Henkels, Louise Fortson, John Rea,
Michael Morris
Marie Caldwell, Gloria McCoy, Penny Allison,
Rose Thompson
Kathleen Saunders, Marianne Sullivan

The Curtis Publishing Company Book Division
Jack Merritt, President
Starkey Flythe, Jr., Editorial Director
David M. Price, Production Manager

First Printing 1978
Second Printing 1979

Contents

Introduction

This book is designed for people who live in small dwellings—apartments, condominiums, ranch houses and mobile homes—where kitchen space is limited and storage space even more so. It is also written for men and women who may have all the space needed for large-scale canning operations but only want to have a few choice items on their shelves and in their freezers.

When harvesttime comes around there is a squirrel-like instinct in most people to take advantage of the oversupply in garden, orchard or market and to store up for winter. Memories of day-long sessions in hot, steaming kitchens such as our mothers and grandmothers used to contend with, when pecks of apples and pears and bushels of tomatoes and corn were brought to the kitchen door to be put up, make most people feel that canning must be done on a wholesale basis or not at all. Not so. It is possible and also enjoyable to can or freeze in small batches.

There are many advantages to canning and freezing fruits and vegetables. Besides the inevitable feeling of smug satisfaction, there is the distinct advantage of knowing the source of these foods and being able to regulate the amount of sugar and salt that is added to them. You can know for a certainty that there are no harmful preservatives and that what you have is a "natural" product. There is increasing evidence that highly refined sugar, when used in large quantities, is injurious to health, and we will suggest ways to avoid using it.

Canning in small quantities is easy and pleasant. In the first place you are doing it because you want to, not because you have to.

In the second place canning or freezing 2 to 4 pints at a time is never tiring and can usually be done along with other kitchen chores. The possibility of error is thus greatly reduced. The prime reason for failure when working with large quantities is that one is tempted to cut corners to save time and both kinds of energy. This is apt to invite disaster.

Finally, canning requires little more equipment than what is found in an everyday kitchen, so that when the spirit moves or when a neighbor drops by with garden extras, it is no bother to pop such produce into can or freezer.

There are certain vegetables and fruits that are more successfully canned than frozen, and others that are better frozen than canned. We will indicate our preference whenever that is the case.

The secret of success is never to overwhelm yourself with large quantities of anything—containers, kettles or produce. Too much will only cause confusion. Buy half-pint and pint jars by the dozen so that you are always prepared. If you have a small cleared area on either side of the sink and another near the stove you may can or freeze with ease. If you lack these, a small table on wheels will make extra work space.

Prepare just 2 to 4 half-pint or pint containers at a time, and before you know it you will have a wonderful array of various fruits and vegetables that will add interest to winter menus.

Canning Methods

Only two methods are acceptable for canning in either large or small quantities: hot-water-bath canning and pressure canning. In addition, open-kettle canning may be used for fruit jellies only. Oven canning and microwave-oven canning do not meet modern standards of safety from deadly botulism or spoilage.

Hot Water Bath Canning

Only high-acid foods (fruits, pickled vegetables and some tomatoes) can safely be processed by the hot-water-bath method. The jars of food are prepared by either the cold-pack or hot-pack procedures, and the lids and closures are put on according to the manufacturer's directions. (We strongly recommend the self-sealing lids and screw bands.) The jars are then placed in a kettle of hot water, on a rack that allows water to circulate under them. A vertical rack is not needed, but there should be space between the jars during processing. Add more hot water as needed to bring the level of the water 1 inch above the lids of the jars. Bring the water to a boil before beginning to count the processing time. When the time is up, remove the jars from the hot water and set them 2 inches apart on a wire rack or on towels, until thoroughly cool. Do not set the hot jars directly on a cool surface or where cool air will blow on them, as the sudden change in temperature may cause the glass to crack.

Pressure Canning

All vegetables other than some tomatoes must be processed under pressure to be absolutely safe. The temperature of boiling water (212 degrees F.) is not hot enough to kill deadly organisms that may dwell in meats, fish and the low-acid vegetables. Steam pressure of 10 pounds indicates that the water inside a pressure cooker is at 240 degrees F., hot enough to make the foods safe if they are processed for the recommended time period.

As an extra precaution, it is recommended that all home-canned low-acid foods be boiled 10 minutes before they are served.

The directions given in this book are intended for use with a pressure *saucepan* rather than the larger and more expensive pressure *canner*. The 6-quart pressure saucepan found in most well-equipped kitchens will process 4 pint jars; you need only provide some kind of rack that

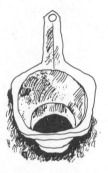

will fit inside it to hold the jars up off the bottom and let water circulate under them. A vertical rack to keep the jars separated is not needed, but the jars should be set well apart so that water and steam can circulate between them.

The pressure saucepan builds up pressure and loses pressure more quickly than the pressure canner; therefore, more time must be allowed for processing. In this book both times are given—the time for processing in the pressure *saucepan* and the shorter time for processing in a pressure *canner*.

Pressure canning instructions will be given with every recipe using that method, but it is wise to review the following guidelines:

PRESSURE CANNING GUIDELINES
Follow these simple steps in using your pressure cooker for canning. Remember, the U.S. Department of Agriculture recommends pressure canning as the ONLY safe method for processing non-acid foods.

(1) Use only jars in perfect condition, free from nicks, cracks and sharp edges. Wash jars and lids in hot sudsy water; rinse thoroughly and let stand in hot water until ready to be used. Follow manufacturer's directions for lids and closures.

(2) Select fresh, firm products and sort according to size and degree of ripeness.

(3) Wash food thoroughly, in several waters if necessary. Lift food out of water in washing.

(4) Fill hot jars with hot food, leaving ½ inch head space for fruits and 1 inch head space for vegetables, such as peas, shelled beans and corn.

(5) Cover with hot liquid as specified. A recipe for the canning bouillon recommended for use with some vegetables is on page 142.

(6) Work out air bubbles with clean plastic or nonmetal rod or knife.

(7) Wipe rim of jar clean of seeds, pulp, juice, etc.

(8) Adjust lids and closures on jars according to directions.

(9) Place rack in pressure cooker. Add 5 cups of boiling water.

(10) Place hot jars on rack in pressure cooker. Turn heat high.

(11) Place cover on pressure cooker and lock in place.

(12) Allow a steady flow of steam to emerge from vent pipe for 5 to 7 minutes.

(13) Place pressure regulator on vent pipe. Start counting processing time as soon as desired pressure is reached. Regulate heat to maintain pressure at required level. Pressure regulator should maintain a slow, steady rocking motion.

(14) Turn off heat at end of processing time and remove the pressure cooker from heat.

(15) Let the pressure return to zero. Do not try to hasten the process by removing the pressure regulator or running cold water over the top or by opening the petcock. This might release the seals on the jars.

(16) When the pressure registers zero, remove the pressure regulator and let the canner stand for 2 minutes. Release the top gradually and lift the cover away from you to prevent any possible scalding by steam.

(17) Remove the jars from the pan and set on a rack or damp towels, leaving space between the jars. Do not move until thoroughly cooled.

Equipment

Small-batch canning requires only the basic equipment of most kitchens, provided that equipment includes a 6-quart pressure cooker with a weighted gauge and a deep 8- to 10-quart kettle, both of which can be used for many kitchen processes other than canning or freezing. Other necessities include a timer, which most stoves are equipped with, a wire trivet and a steamer or, best of all, a collapsible metal lettuce drier with little legs which can be used as a steamer when preparing the fruits and vegetables and for processing canned fruits and vegetables.

Treat yourself to good new jars and closures. This insures success and increases your satisfaction in the finished product. We recommend

particularly the self-adhesive tops and the screw bands which can be used over and over again once the lids are securely affixed to the jars.

To make sure of a good seal, fill the jar just to the level recommended in the directions. Wipe the rim of the jar and screw threads with a clean, damp cloth or with paper toweling to remove any juice or pulp, before putting on the lid and screw band. Screw the band on firmly by hand but do not use a wrench or any other device to tighten it. Some air will be exhausted from the jar during processing, and a vacuum will form as the jar and its contents cool. Do not tighten or loosen the screw band immediately after processing. After 24 hours you can remove the screw band and use it again on another jar.

Little inexpensive extras such as a ladle, a stainless steel tea ball, jar tongs and a jelly thermometer make the process neater and easier and are well worth the investment.

Canning Do's

(1) Clear and wash all working surfaces. Cleanliness is the sure road to success.

(2) Check and clean all necessary equipment. The easiest way is to run everything through the dishwasher just before canning, including measuring cups and spoons, knives, spoons, ladles, jars, lids and closures. Keep the jars in the dishwasher until you are ready to fill them. Otherwise, wash everything in hot, soapy water, rinse well and keep the jars, lids and rings in hot water.

(3) Process vegetables and fruits quickly after they have been picked. The rule of thumb is 2 hours from garden to jar. Obviously this is not always possible, but the quicker the better. Some vegetables are better canned than frozen; other vegetables are better frozen than canned. Each fruit and vegetable recipe will indicate the preferred method if there is a preference.

(4) Sort fruits and vegetables according to size and can them accordingly.

(5) Wash vegetables thoroughly, using several changes of water if necessary both before and, in most cases, after preparing for canning.

(6) Follow the directions carefully for each fruit and vegetable.

Canning Don'ts

(1) Don't waste your time on anything but perfect fruits and vegetables. Canning does not *improve* produce, so start with the best.

(2) Don't let fruits and vegetables soak in water. Valuable vitamins and minerals will be washed away.

(3) Don't get too far from the kitchen when you are using the pressure saucepan. If the rubber gasket has been checked and the petcock and safety valve are clear you will have no trouble, but plan to do something nearby, just in case.

Storage

Storage in a small dwelling is always a problem. Canned goods—whether they be fruits, vegetables, jams, jellies or pickles—are best kept in a cool, dark place (under 70 degrees F.). Assuming that there is neither a cellar nor attic in your home, the best solution is a closet or cupboard somewhat removed from stove or fireplace. If there is a closet or part of a closet in any part of the house that can be saved for food storage, its capacity can be greatly increased by installing small shelves, 2 jars deep and 6 or 7 inches apart, on closet wall or door. If necessary the door can be weather stripped to keep out the heat. If closet space is too precious, save the boxes the jars come in and pack the jars, once filled, into the boxes and stash them wherever possible, but this is not as satisfactory as seeing pretty jars decoratively labeled arranged on a shelf.

Freezing Vegetables and Fruits

A freezer may still be considered a luxury by some, but in our estimation it is a luxury that borders on necessity if one is to take advantage of the convenience, the safety and the satisfaction it provides. The size of a freezer depends on space and number of people it is to service. Good planning makes even a small freezer a worthwhile investment. Some vegetables and fruits are better canned than frozen or vice versa. In some cases both are equally good. Each recipe will indicate our judgment.

Containers: The markets are full of containers and wrappings for freezing, most of them very satisfactory. The purpose is that they should protect the food so that it will retain its garden-fresh color, taste and texture. For rigid containers we recommend the ½-pint, 1-pint, 1½-pint containers with straight bottoms, sides and tops, just because they pack easily in the freezer and stack well in the cupboard. The glass jars made for freezing are decorative and useful for gifts. For nonrigid containers there are heavy plastic bags that can be most easily filled if placed first in a plastic box. Pack the food according to the directions in each recipe. When using rigid containers it is important to leave ample head space to allow for expansion. The covers must be pressed firmly into place. When using plastic bags it is important to press out as much air as possible before sealing them with a heating tool (available in any hardware store) or by using metal twistems.

Labeling and Storing. Write the name and date for freezing containers on masking tape and place on top so that the label is easily readable. This saves the covers for future use. Once the vegetables are sealed put them in the freezer at once. For quick freezing place the containers apart from one another for 24 hours to allow the air to circulate. When frozen they may be packed close together.

Fast freezing means that moisture in the food turns into tiny crystals, best preserving the natural texture and flavor of the food.

Slow freezing produces large-size crystals that break down the cell walls in fruits or vegetables, so that the thawed product is less satisfactory.

Keep in mind that freezing stops the growth of the organisms that cause spoilage but does not kill them as high heat does in the canning process. Once the food becomes warm again, the organisms begin to grow and multiply. This can happen during a power failure, or if your freezer is accidentally disconnected from the electrical outlet. Partially thawed foods should be cooked or canned immediately, or they should be destroyed. Do not refreeze thawed foods, and if there is any doubt about their safety, don't allow anyone to eat them.

It is helpful to keep an inventory of frozen foods that can be checked off as fruits and vegetables are used. You will find it easier to check the inventory list than to rummage through the entire freezer when you need to know what's available.

Basic Steps for Freezing Vegetables

(1) Use only vegetables that are young and freshly picked.

(2) Wash and prepare the vegetables according to directions in individual recipes.

(3) "Blanch" or boil vegetables according to directions. This is to stop the action of enzymes which make the vegetables grow. If enzyme action is allowed to continue, the vegetable can become coarse and flavorless. Enzymes defy freezing but cannot withstand heat. Follow the prescribed timing. If you live more than 5,000 feet above sea level add 1 minute to the directions.

(4) Once the vegetables are blanched they should be immediately drained and plunged into cold running water or ice water. The advantage of freezing vegetables in small batches is that you are not tempted to cool too much at one time. Allow the same amount of time for cooling as for blanching. Drain thoroughly and follow directions for packing.

(5) Freezer temperature should be 0 degrees F.

Basic Steps for Freezing Fruits

(1) Use fruit that is at its peak of perfection.

(2) Wash quickly in cold water.

(3) Prepare the fruit according to directions, using ascorbic acid to prevent discoloration when necessary.

(4) Measure and prepare the dry sugar or syrup for sweetening unless the fruit is to be packed without sweetening.

(5) Pack in rigid containers or plastic bags according to directions.

(6) Place containers in freezer apart from each other so as to permit air circulation and consequent quick freezing.

(7) Freezer temperature should be 0 degrees F.

Canning and
Freezing Vegetables

Vegetables, whether they be home-canned or home-frozen, can be the basis for many meals—both family style and party fare. Not only do you have the satisfaction of knowing how and where they were grown, but there is a certain joy in knowing you are beating the budget at least in that department. Preparing them yourself allows you to regulate the amount of sugar and salt if that is a consideration in the family diet. Experiments show that neither salt nor sugar affects the preserving of the vegetables although it does, of course, vary the flavor slightly. Follow the directions for preserving, and when the time comes to use the vegetables, try the recipes that are suggested on these pages.

Asparagus

Canned or frozen asparagus is a pleasant change in the middle of winter. The frozen variety has a fresher taste but the canned is excellent in soups, soufflés or in the recipe given below. Cook the canned asparagus 10 minutes in boiling water before using; the frozen variety can be cooked just 3 to 5 minutes according to the size of the stalks. Allow 1½ to 2 pounds of fresh asparagus for a pint of canned or frozen. Have your work area cleared and your equipment ready before obtaining the asparagus.

Buy or pick asparagus spears of equal thickness. The shorter the time between garden and canner, the better the product will be.

Wash the asparagus and cut off the tough ends. Unless the asparagus is very young, peel off the scales with a potato peeler. Wash again.

CANNING

Cold Pack: Cut the asparagus the length of the jars minus ½ inch. Pile them in, holding the jar almost on its side for easy packing. Or, cut the spears in 1-inch lengths and pack them in so that the jar is well filled but not crowded. Fill to within ½ inch of the top with boiling water. Add ½ teaspoon of salt if desired. Adjust the lids and closures. Process 45 minutes in a pressure saucepan, 25 minutes in a pressure canner.

Remove the jars from the canner and let them stand well apart to cool completely, then label and store.

Hot Pack: Steam the asparagus spears for 3 minutes, standing them upright in boiling water which comes to within 1 inch of the tips of the asparagus. Or cut them in 1-inch pieces and boil for 2 minutes. Drain and save the water.

Pack the hot vegetables into the jars. Lay asparagus spears in with tips up, or fill the jars not too tightly with cut-up asparagus pieces. Cover with the hot asparagus water up to within ½ inch of the top. Add boiling water if necessary. Proceed as in directions for the Cold Pack.

FREEZING

Cut the asparagus into 1-inch pieces if they are to be used in soups, soufflés or in creamed sauce. Otherwise cut the spears the length of the containers they are to be stored in (freezer boxes or jars). Sort the asparagus according to thickness.

Blanch the asparagus in boiling water, no more than 1 pound at a time, allowing 1½ minutes for the thin variety, 2 to 3 minutes for the thicker spears. Drain and plunge into ice water. Remove with a slotted spatula to paper toweling and pat dry. Pack in plastic bags, making sure the tips are at the bottom of the bag. If using regular jars, alternate tips and ends for closer packing. If using the wide-mouthed jars, put all the tips at the bottom. Seal and label. Place in the coldest part of the freezer with space between the jars or bags. After 24 hours they can be packed more closely.

Ham and Asparagus Pie

1 9-inch pie shell	1 cup milk
1 pint canned or frozen asparagus	Salt and pepper
4 tablespoons butter or margarine	¼ pound boiled ham, sliced paper thin
4 tablespoons unbleached or whole wheat pastry flour	2 hard-cooked eggs
¾ teaspoon Dijon mustard	¾ cup grated Gruyère or mild Cheddar cheese

Prepare and bake a pie shell according to your favorite recipe, or purchase one from the freezing section of your local market.

If using canned asparagus, boil vigorously for 10 minutes, using the canning liquid. Cook frozen asparagus in ¼ cup of lightly salted water just until tender. Drain the asparagus but save the cooking liquid.

Preheat the oven to 375 degrees F.

Heat the butter or margarine and whisk in the flour, stirring for 1 minute. Add the mustard, the milk and ¾ cup of the cooking liquid. Stir until thick and smooth and season to taste with salt and pepper.

Arrange half the asparagus in the pie shell. Spoon over a third of the sauce. Shred the ham over the surface and cover with slices of hard-cooked egg. Spoon another third of sauce over the eggs. Cover with the remaining asparagus. Spread the remaining third of sauce over the asparagus and sprinkle with grated cheese.

Bake the pie 10 to 15 minutes or until bubbling hot. If the top is not golden brown, turn on the broiler for a few moments.

Serves 4 to 6 persons.

Beans—Lima Beans

Lima beans can be preserved by canning or freezing. Select well-filled pods. The beans should be green and not overly plump or yellowed in color. Discard any beans that have yellowed. Two to 2½ pounds of lima beans in the pods will yield 1 pint of canned or frozen beans. Preserved lima beans are slightly bland in flavor but can be cooked in a variety of delicious ways. They are rich in nutrients and can be used as a meat substitute.

Shell the lima beans and then wash them, lifting from the water so that any grit will be left at the bottom of the pan. Separate the beans according to size if necessary.

CANNING

Cold Pack: Pack raw, washed beans into clean jars to within 1 inch from top if the beans are small, to ¾ inch if large. Do not shake or press the beans down. Add ½ teaspoon of salt if desired.

Fill the jars with boiling water or canning bouillon to within ½ inch from the top, and run a nonmetal rod around the edge to release any air bubbles. Adjust the lid tops.

Process in pressure saucepan at 10 pounds pressure for 60 minutes, or in a pressure canner 40 minutes. Remove the jars and cool on a rack or towel with plenty of air space between the jars. Label and store.

Hot Pack: Shell and wash the beans, cover with boiling water and bring to a boil.

Pack hot beans *loosely* to within 1 inch of the top, adding ½ teaspoon of salt if desired.

Cover with boiling water or canning bouillon to within 1 inch of the top. Run a nonmetal rod around edge of jar to release any air bubbles.

Adjust the lids and process as for Cold Pack.

Remove jars from canner and place on a rack to cool, leaving plenty of air space between the jars. Label and store when completely cooled.

FREEZING

Shell and wash the beans. Sort according to size if necessary. Discard any beans that are overdeveloped or have turned yellowish.

Blanch small beans in boiling water for 2 minutes; for medium beans

allow 3 minutes; for large beans 4 minutes. Immediately plunge the beans into cold or iced water. Drain.

Pack into containers, leaving ½ inch head space. Seal, label and freeze.

Beans—Snap, Green or Yellow Wax Beans

Green and yellow wax beans are preserved and cooked in the same way. Sometimes it makes a pretty effect to cook them together, although the green variety is usually preferred to its paler cousin because it has more flavor. We particularly recommend the so-called Italian bean, which is slightly flatter in shape. The specter of botulism is sometimes associated with canned green beans, but there is no danger if the beans are processed properly in a pressure canner or pressure saucepan.

Canned or frozen beans dressed in a vinaigrette sauce and covered with thinly sliced raw onions make a delicious winter salad. Or served hot in a cheesy mushroom sauce or with toasted slivered almonds in a butter sauce, they make a wonderful accompaniment to almost any entree. For a special occasion try Green Beans Extraordinary.

Three to 4 pounds of beans, depending on their maturity, will yield 4 pints of canned or frozen beans. Choose young, tender beans. Wash them well and sort according to size if necessary. Use a sharp knife or kitchen scissors to cut off the tips. If small and tender, leave them whole; otherwise cut into 2- to 3-inch lengths. Wash again.

CANNING

Cold Pack: Pack the prepared beans tightly into jars, leaving ½ inch head space. Fill with boiling water or canning bouillon, adding ½ teaspoon of salt if desired. Adjust the lids and closures. Process 40 minutes at 10 pounds pressure in a pressure saucepan (if using a pressure canner process 20 minutes). Let the pressure return to normal.

Remove the jars. Let them cool on a towel with air space between. Remove the screw bands before labeling and storing. They are reusable.

Hot Pack: Place the prepared beans in boiling water to cover. (If the beans are in a steamer basket, they will be easier to retrieve.) Boil 5 minutes. Pack the beans (not too tightly) into the hot jars, using a spoon. Leave 1 inch head space. Fill the jars with the bean water or boiling canning bouillon to within ½ inch of the top. Adjust the lids and closures and process as for Cold Pack.

FREEZING

Blanch 2 cups of the prepared beans at a time, using the steaming basket. Count 3 minutes after the water returns to a boil. Plunge into ice cold water for 2 minutes. Drain and turn onto toweling to dry. Pack into pint plastic bags, boxes or jars, leaving ½ inch head space. Seal, label and freeze in coldest part of the freezer, leaving space between the containers until completely frozen (24 hours).

Green Beans Extraordinary

1 pint canned or frozen green beans	1 cup bean sprouts (home grown or canned)
½ cup chopped onion	¾ cup chopped cashews
2 tablespoons butter or margarine	1 cup chicken broth
	1 cup sour cream

Boil the beans in the canning liquid for 10 minutes, or in ¼ cup of slightly salted water just until tender if using the frozen beans. Drain.

Meanwhile, sauté the onion in the butter or margarine just until the onion is tender. Add the bean sprouts and cashews and toss until mixed. Add the beans and continue cooking and tossing for 1 minute. Add the chicken broth. Cover and cook 10 minutes. Remove from the stove. Add the sour cream and season to taste. Reheat without boiling.

Serves 4 persons.

Beans—Horticultural or Shell

Shell beans are the beans found in the pod after the string or wax beans have been allowed to ripen on the vine. The pod, while still moist, is thin and papery and easy to shell. Modern seed merchants have hybridized and grown seeds that are meant for the shelled variety alone. These beans are often used for "Baked Beans," but they can also be prepared in other ways. Rich in protein and iron, they make an excellent meat substitute and can be preserved by canning, freezing or drying, though drying isn't practical in the small kitchen. Two and one-half to 3½ pounds of shelled beans in their pods will yield 3 pints of shelled beans, depending on size and fullness of the pods.

CANNING

Cold Pack: Shell the beans and wash them well. Drain and pack loosely into pint jars, leaving 1 inch head space. Shell beans will expand in cooking. Add boiling water just to cover. Add ½ teaspoon of canning salt if desired. Adjust the lids and closures. Process the jars for 60 minutes at 10 pounds of pressure in a pressure saucepan or 40 minutes in a pressure canner.

Hot Pack: Put the washed and shelled beans in a pan. Cover with water and bring to a boil. Drain the liquid into another saucepan and save. Fill the pint jars loosely to within 1 inch of the top. Cover with the hot bean liquid, adding more boiling water if necessary. Adjust the lids and closures and process as for Cold Pack.

FREEZING

Blanch the beans, using only the small and small-to-medium size. Boil 2 minutes for the smaller beans and 2½ minutes for those slightly larger. Drain and plunge into cold water. Package in pint plastic containers, flexible bags or freezing jars.

Horticultural Beans in Cream

Horticultural beans are admittedly caloric. They are also nutritious and very delicious. To our way of thinking they demand a solo appearance at luncheon or supper with nothing else except dark buttered bread and applesauce.

1 pint canned horticultural beans Cream	Salt and freshly ground black pepper

Boil the beans in their canning liquid until the beans are soft (about 15 minutes), adding water if necessary.

When ready to serve, most of the liquid should have evaporated. Add ¼ to ½ cup of heavy cream. Season well with salt and black pepper.

Beets

Large beets can be cooked, sliced or cubed and then canned or frozen; but when space is limited, we prefer to can only small beets. Beets can be decorative as well as delicious. Eight pounds of small red or yellow beets (measured without the tops) should yield 4 pints of the canned variety. Buy or dig beets of uniformly small size, about 1½ inches in diameter.

CANNING

Beets must be cooked before canning, so only the Hot Pack method is recommended. Cut off all but about 1 inch of the tops and leave the roots on. Wash gently but thoroughly, leaving the skins intact. Boil in a pan of salted water to which a teaspoon of vinegar has been added. This will keep the color bright. Cook 15 to 20 minutes or until the beets are tender when pierced with a fork. Drain and cool enough to handle.

Trim the stem and the root ends and peel off the skin.

Pack the beets into clean, hot pint jars. Tap the jars gently on the working surface to settle the beets, and allow room for a few more. Leave ½ inch head space at the top of the jar.

Fill each jar with boiling water up to within ½ inch of the top. Run a nonmetal blade around the edge of each jar to release air bubbles. Add more boiling water to reach the ½-inch mark.

Put on the lids and closures, according to manufacturers' directions. Process at 10 pounds of pressure for 50 minutes in a pressure saucepan, 30 minutes in a pressure canner.

Remove jars from the canner and let stand 2 inches apart until cool.

Honeyed Beets

Use the canned beets for this recipe. It is a delicious accompaniment to roast pork or game.

1	pint small whole beets	½	teaspoon salt
2	tablespoons butter or margarine	3	tablespoons honey
		¾	cup orange juice
2	tablespoons flour	1	tablespoon lemon juice

Boil the beets for 10 minutes.

Melt the butter or margarine and stir in the flour. When they are well blended, stir in the salt, honey, orange and lemon juice. Continue stirring until the sauce thickens.

Add the beets, stir well and simmer until the beets are heated through.

Serves 4 persons.

Broccoli

Broccoli, like other members of the cabbage family, does not lend itself to canning as well as it does to freezing, and we do not recommend using up limited storage space with the canned variety. However, the frozen variety can be served as a sauced or buttered vegetable, in soups and purees, soufflés and ring molds and is particularly good in fritters. One pound of broccoli will yield 1 pint of frozen, which will serve 2 to 3 people. In small kitchens do not process more than 4 pounds at a time. Divide the broccoli so that you blanch no more than 1 pound at a time.

FREEZING

If you are harvesting your own broccoli, cut the tightly budded green heads from the stalk with not more than 2 inches of stem. The stalk will continue to produce more heads. If buying broccoli, try to find freshly picked dark green bunches with no sign of yellow flowers.

Trim the leaves and large stalks from the broccoli. Divide the broccoli into bunches about 1 inch in diameter with tender stems.

Soak the broccoli in a bowl containing 2 quarts of water mixed with ½ cup of salt for 15 minutes. Drain and place in a steaming basket. Plunge into boiling water for 3 minutes. Drain and cool in a pan of iced water for 3 minutes. Drain and dry on paper toweling. Pack into containers, leaving no head room. Seal and freeze.

Broccoli Fritters

Broccoli fritters go well with grilled steak or chops and can be cooked at the same time. The new small deep-fat fryers or an electric skillet will do very well in the absence of a regular deep-fat fryer. The secret is to have the oil very hot (380 degrees F.) so that the food absorbs a minimum of oil while cooking. Prepare the broccoli and the batter in advance.

1 pint frozen broccoli	½ teaspoon salt
1 egg yolk, well beaten	4-5 ounces flat beer
2 teaspoons salad oil	1 egg white, beaten
⅔ cup unbleached flour	stiff (optional)

Leave the broccoli in its container at room temperature for about 1½ hours. Divide into flowerets and steam in 4 tablespoons of water in a covered pan for 3 minutes or until barely tender. Drain the separated flowerets on paper toweling.

Combine the egg yolk, salad oil, flour and salt with enough beer to make a heavy cream consistency. Cover the bowl and refrigerate for at least 3 hours. The addition of the beaten egg white just before using will produce a lighter fritter.

Preheat the fat to 380 degrees F.

Dip each well-dried floweret into the batter, using a long-handled fork. Shake gently to remove excess batter. Drop the floweret into the fat. Repeat the process quickly until you have 4 or 5 fritters cooking. Turn each one after 1 minute of cooking. Fry 1 to 2 minutes longer, depending on the size of the floweret. Remove and drain on paper toweling. Keep warm in a slightly opened warm oven until the broccoli fritters are all cooked. Salt lightly and serve immediately.

Brussels Sprouts

Brussels sprouts are best preserved by freezing. One pound will yield 1 pint of frozen sprouts.

FREEZING

Choose only the bright green heads, and sort them according to size for blanching and freezing.

Wash them well, removing any loose leaves and trimming the bottom stems. Blanch in a kettle of boiling water, allowing 3 minutes for the smaller size, 4 minutes for medium size and 5 minutes for the large sprouts. Drain and throw into very cold—preferably iced—water. Let stand 3 to 6 minutes or until well chilled. Drain and dry on paper toweling. Pack into containers, leaving no head room. Seal and freeze.

Brussels Sprouts au Gratin

This dish is better prepared in advance, just because cooking any member of the cabbage family can be unappetizingly odoriferous.

1 pint frozen Brussels sprouts	½ cup heavy cream
1 cup chicken broth	3 tablespoons fine seasoned bread crumbs
2½ tablespoons butter or margarine	Salt and pepper
2 tablespoons unbleached flour	Nutmeg

Combine the sprouts and chicken broth in a small saucepan. Cover and bring to a rapid boil. Boil 2 minutes. Remove the cover and cook 3 minutes longer or until just tender. Drain the liquid into another saucepan and boil down until the liquid measures approximately 1 cup.

Put the sprouts into a small (1 quart) oven-serving dish.

Heat 2 tablespoons of butter or margarine in the original saucepan. Blend in the flour. Cook 1 minute. Add the reduced broth and whisk until smooth. Add the cream and season with salt, pepper and a dash of nutmeg.

Pour the sauce over the sprouts.

Sprinkle the top with the bread crumbs and dot with the remaining butter.

Before serving, bake the sprouts for 20 minutes at 350 degrees F. If you have a single oven which is being used for a roast at a different temperature, don't fret. The sprouts can be reheated for a longer or shorter time at any reasonable temperature. If the top is not sufficiently browned, slip the dish under the broiler for a few minutes.

Serves 3 to 4 persons.

Carrots

Since you are going to preserve only a few carrots, take the time to cut them into small matchsticks, unless you have uniformly sized and slender new carrots. In that way they will be decorative for cold salads or in hot vegetable dishes. Young carrots can be canned or frozen, but canning seems to produce better results.

Buy or pull young carrots. You can always buy the big variety in the market. One and one-fourth to 1½ pounds of carrots (without tops) will yield 1 pint of canned or frozen carrots.

Wash and scrape the carrots. Cut them into small sticks about 2 inches long.

CANNING

Cold Pack: Pack carrots tightly into hot pint jars. Add ½ teaspoon of canning salt, if desired. Pour in boiling water to within ½ inch from the top. Run a wooden or plastic blade around the edge of the jar to release air bubbles. Add more boiling water to bring it up to the ½-inch mark. Put on the lids and closures. Process pint jars in the pressure saucepan at 10 pounds pressure for 45 minutes, in the pressure canner 25 minutes. Cool the jars, letting them stand at least 2 inches apart from one another. Label and store.

Hot Pack: Prepare the carrots as above. Put in a saucepan and cover with boiling water. Boil 1 minute. Remove the carrot sticks from the pan with a slotted spoon to hot, clean jars, filling to within ½ inch of the top. Add the boiling carrot water and enough extra boiling water to come within ½ inch of the top. Proceed as in the directions for Cold Pack.

Carrots in Cointreau

This is a delicious accompaniment to baked ham and can be prepared in a matter of minutes.

1 pint canned matchstick carrots	½ teaspoon salt
4 tablespoons water	2 tablespoons sugar
3 tablespoons butter or margarine	1 teaspoon lemon juice
	2 tablespoons Cointreau

Drain the canned carrots.

Combine the water, butter, sugar and salt in a small, shallow saucepan.

Bring to a boil and add the carrots. Cook over moderate heat for 5 to 8 minutes or until almost all the moisture has disappeared.

Remove from the heat and add the lemon juice and Cointreau. Stir until well mixed. Serve hot.

Serves 2 to 4 persons.

Cauliflower

Cauliflower may be frozen for use as a cooked vegetable. It does not lend itself to canning very satisfactorily except as pickles.

Select tender, snow-white heads, knifing off any small brown imperfections. Two medium-size heads will yield 3 pint containers of frozen cauliflower.

FREEZING

Soak the heads in a salt and water solution (4 teaspoons of salt to each gallon of water) for 30 minutes to remove any insects.

Break into flowerets and cut away the large stalks.

Break or cut the flowerets into pieces about 1 inch across.

Blanch for 3 minutes in boiling water to which 4 teaspoons of salt per gallon have been added.

Plunge immediately into cold or iced water.

Pack the cauliflower into containers loosely, leaving no head space. Seal and freeze.

Neapolitan Cauliflower

This dish, born of hard times during the war in Italy, comes from an Italian lady who was a magician at serving a large family generously even when food supplies were very low.

2 pints frozen cauliflower	2 cups milk
4 tablespoons butter or margarine	1 cup grated Cheddar cheese
4 tablespoons unbleached or whole wheat pastry flour	1 cup cubed salami (4 ounces)
	Salt and pepper

Thaw the cauliflower to the extent that the flowerets separate easily. Place the bite-size pieces in a baking-serving dish.

Heat the butter or margarine in a saucepan. Whisk in the flour and cook over low heat for 1 or 2 minutes. Add the milk and whisk constantly until the sauce is smooth and thick. Add the grated cheese and continue whisking until the cheese is melted. Remove from the heat.

Buy the salami in 1 piece and cut into ½-inch slices and then into cubes. Stir the salami into the sauce. Season to taste with salt and pepper.

Cover the thawed or partially thawed cauliflower with the sauce.

Bake 20 minutes at 350 degrees F. Turn the broiler on for the last few minutes to make a brown crusty top.

Serves 6 persons.

Corn

Corn cans and freezes well. It should be fresh from the garden; prompt processing insures highest flavor. Two to 2½ pounds in husks yield one pint of canned or frozen corn. It may be processed as cream-style or whole-kernel corn. Canning corn requires long processing and therefore more fuel energy in preparation, but no energy to store—so make your own choice.

Select ears with plump, tender kernels and thin, sweet milk. If the milk is thick and starchy, it is better to process the corn as cream-style.

Husk the corn, remove the silk and wash the ears.

CANNING

Cream-Style Cold Pack: Cut corn from the cob at about center of kernel and scrape the cobs.

Pack corn to within 1½ inches of top; do not shake or press down. Add ½ teaspoon of salt if desired.

Fill with boiling water to within ½ inch of top, running a nonmetal rod around edge to release any air bubbles.

Adjust the jar lids.

Process in pressure saucepan at 10 pounds pressure for 1 hour and 55 minutes (95 minutes with standard pressure canner).

Remove jars from canner and allow them to cool on a towel or rack, leaving plenty of air space between the jars.

Label and store.

Cream-Style Hot Pack: Cut corn from cob at about the center of the kernels and scrape the cobs.

To each pint of corn add 1 cup of boiling water.

Boil 3 minutes.

Pack the hot corn in its liquid to within 1 inch of the top, adding ½ teaspoon of salt if desired.

Adjust the jar lids.

Process in pressure saucepan at 10 pounds pressure for 1 hour and 45 minutes (85 minutes for standard pressure canner).

Remove jars from canner and allow them to cool on a rack or towel, leaving plenty of air space between the jars.

Label and store.

Whole-Kernel Cold Pack: Cut the corn from the cob at about ⅔ the depth of the kernels.

Pack the corn to within 1 inch of the top without shaking or pressing down. Add, if desired, ½ teaspoon of salt to each pint.

Fill the jars with boiling water to within ½ inch of top, running a nonmetal rod around the jar to release any air bubbles.

Adjust the lids.

Process in pressure saucepan at 10 pounds pressure for 1 hour and 15 minutes (55 minutes for standard pressure canner).

Remove the jars and place them on a towel or rack to cool, leaving plenty of air space between the jars.

Label and store.

Whole-Kernel Hot Pack: Cut from the cob at about ⅔ the depth of the kernel.

To each pint of corn add 1 cup of boiling water and reheat to boiling.

Pack hot corn with the liquid to within 1 inch of top, adding ½ teaspoon of salt if desired.

Adjust the lids.

Process in pressure saucepan at 10 pounds pressure for 1 hour and 15 minutes (55 minutes in standard pressure canner).

Remove the jars and set on a rack or towel to cool, leaving plenty of air space between the jars.

Label and store.

FREEZING

Heat the husked and washed ears in boiling water for 4 to 6 minutes, depending on size. Plunge into cold or iced water and drain.

Cut kernels from cob at about ⅔ the depth of the kernels.

Pack corn into containers, leaving ½ inch head space.

Seal and freeze.

Golden Corn Bisque

This soup, made of cream-style corn, can be served covered with fresh popcorn to make a hearty luncheon dish for 4 people. Served in bouillon cups garnished with lightly salted whipped cream and flecks of chopped parsley, it makes a delicious beginning to a dinner party for 8.

1 pint cream-style corn (canned or thawed frozen)	2½ cups milk Salt and white pepper
1 pint water	GARNISH:
½ cup sliced onion	Popped corn or ½ cup heavy cream, whipped
3 tablespoons butter	
3 tablespoons flour	

Combine the corn, water and onion in a saucepan. Bring to a boil. Cover and simmer 10 minutes.

Meanwhile, heat the butter or margarine in the top of a double boiler over direct heat. Whisk in the flour, and, when it is well blended, add the milk and whisk until smooth. Place the pan over simmering water.

Spin the corn mixture in a blender or food processor until smooth, or force through a food mill. Add to the contents of the double boiler.

Season to taste with salt and pepper. Cover and simmer 20 to 30 minutes.

Garnish as desired.

Serves 4 to 8 persons.

Corn Pudding

Corn pudding is a meal in itself or makes an excellent accompaniment to baked ham. Eaten in midwinter, it evokes pleasant memories of summertime's fresh corn.

2 tablespoons butter or margarine	1 pint whole-kernel corn (canned or frozen)
4 tablespoons chopped onion (fresh or frozen)	3 eggs
	2 cups milk
4 tablespoons chopped pepper (fresh or frozen)	1 teaspoon salt
	¼ teaspoon white pepper
	Parsley

Preheat the oven to 350 degrees F. Place a cake tin, 2 inches deep, in the oven, half filled with water.

Butter a 1-quart oven-serving dish.

Heat the butter or margarine in a small skillet. Sauté the onion and pepper just until the onion is tender but not brown. Remove from the heat.

Drain the corn if you are using the canned variety. Thaw the frozen variety to the extent that the kernels are separate. Stir the kernels into the onion mixture.

Beat the eggs and milk until blended. Add the salt and pepper.

Stir in the vegetables and pour the mixture into the prepared baking dish.

Place the dish in the pan of hot water. Bake for 50 minutes. Before serving, garnish with sprigs of fresh parsley.

Serves 6 persons.

Eggplant

We recommend freezing eggplant ready for use in prepared dishes such as the casseroles the Italians and Greeks excel in. Moussaka is a Mediterranean favorite. We like to make the eggplant base for Moussaka and freeze it; a full meal is then at our fingertips, with nothing to do but add cheeses, eggs and the white sauce (which can also be prepared in advance and frozen).

Frozen Moussaka Base

6	cups (1½ pounds) eggplant (peeled and cubed)	1	pound ground beef or lamb
3	tablespoons butter or margarine	1½	tablespoons tomato paste
3	tablespoons oil	½	cup red wine
1	cup chopped onion	½	teaspoon cinnamon
1	clove garlic, minced	1½	teaspoons salt
		½	teaspoon pepper

Prepare the eggplant as quickly as possible and sauté immediately in 1 tablespoon of butter and 3 tablespoons of oil for 5 minutes, stirring gently until lightly browned on all sides. Remove from the skillet with a slotted spoon.

Add 2 more tablespoons of butter to the skillet and sauté the onion and garlic just until tender.

Add the meat and stir with a fork until all the red color disappears. Stir in the tomato paste, which has been previously blended with the wine. Add the eggplant, cinnamon, salt and pepper. Stir until the mixture boils. Cover and reduce the heat. Simmer 30 minutes. Cool thoroughly. Pack into pint freezing boxes or jars, leaving ½ inch head space. Seal, label and freeze.

Yields 2 pints.

Moussaka

1 pint moussaka base, thawed	2 eggs, slightly beaten
4 tablespoons butter or margarine	2 tablespoons chopped parsley
4 tablespoons unbleached flour or whole wheat pastry flour	Salt and pepper
2 cups milk	½ cup grated Greek cheese (Kefaloteri) or Parmesan
1 cup drained cottage cheese (cream style)	4 tablespoons fine bread crumbs

Heat the butter or margarine. Whisk in the flour, and, when it is well blended, add the milk and whisk until thick and smooth. Remove from the heat and cool for 5 minutes.

Add the cottage cheese, previously mixed with the eggs. Whisk vigorously. Add the parsley and season with salt and pepper.

Preheat the oven to 350 degrees F.

Butter a quart-size oven-serving dish. Spread a layer of half the thawed eggplant mixture on the bottom of the dish. Cover with half the sauce. Sprinkle with bread crumbs and then with half the grated cheese. Repeat the process. Place the dish on a baking sheet and bake 40 minutes. Remove from the oven and let stand 10 minutes before serving.

Serve with crusty bread and a green salad.

Serves 4 persons.

Mushrooms

When mushrooms flood the market at comparatively low prices, it is hard to resist buying a large basket and processing them for future use. Freezing is the best method (except for pickling mushrooms). For highest flavor we advise precooking them in butter, either whole or in duxelles form, which is a good way to take care of the stems. Do not wash the mushrooms unless absolutely necessary.

Trim and remove the stems. Brush the caps clean with a baby's toothbrush or a special brush made of goose feathers (available in specialty stores).

FREEZING

Pan-Broiled Mushroom Caps: Choose mushrooms of approximately the same size or sort them according to size.

Trim and remove the stems and use them for duxelles (see Frozen Standbys).

For every 2 cups of mushrooms allow 1½ tablespoons of butter and 1½ tablespoons of salad oil.

Heat the fat in a small skillet. Add the mushrooms and sauté 2 minutes on each side. Place in a ½-pint container. Cool and chill. Cover, label and freeze.

If the mushrooms do not fill the container, fill the air space with crumpled wax paper.

Whole Mushrooms: Trim and remove the stems. Clean the caps and place them on a baking sheet, allowing space between each cap. Place in the freezer for 12 hours. Store in ½-pint containers.

Remove the mushrooms from the freezer only a short time before they are to be used; do not let them thaw completely.

Mushrooms sur Croûte

This makes a great luncheon or supper dish.

1 pint frozen mushrooms	4 large slices Italian bread
½ pint cream	1 teaspoon Worcestershire
2 tablespoons butter or	sauce (optional)
margarine	Salt and pepper
4 ¼-inch slices of	Parsley
precooked ham	

Heat the partially thawed mushrooms in the cream without letting them boil. Season with salt and pepper and Worcestershire sauce if desired.

Heat the butter in a skillet and sauté the ham slices on both sides just until heated through. Transfer to a plate.

Sauté the bread slices in the same skillet so that they are golden brown.

To assemble: Put the bread on individual heated plates. Cover with the ham and then with mushrooms. Garnish with a sprig of parsley and serve immediately.

Serves 4 persons.

Okra

Okra is one of the vegetables that should be given shelf or freezer space only if the family enjoys it. Some people do—some people don't. Okra is excellent in stews and gumbos, and we recommend it for all such dishes. Whole boiled okra served with hollandaise sauce is delicious when the okra is fresh from the garden, but the canned or frozen variety tastes better when playing a minor part in a very good dish. About ¾ pound of okra will yield 1 pint canned or frozen.

Select young green pods no longer than 3 inches. Wash thoroughly and cut off the stems without removing the ends.

CANNING

Parboil in plenty of water for 1 minute. Drain and cut in 1-inch pieces, using a sharp knife or kitchen scissors. Discard the cap end.

Fill pint jars to within ½ inch of the top and barely cover with boiling water. Add ½ teaspoon of canning salt if desired. Process in the pressure saucepan at 10 pounds pressure for 45 minutes. Allow 25 minutes if using the standard pressure canner.

FREEZING

Wash the small pods very thoroughly, removing the stems but not the pod ends. Blanch 3 minutes in boiling water. Plunge into very cold water and let stand 2 minutes. Cut in slices and pack in ½-pint or pint containers, leaving ½ inch head space. Discard the pod caps. Seal, label and freeze.

Instant Gumbo

It's possible to prepare this dish very quickly with most of the ingredients coming from your freezer or canning cupboard. If you fry a slice or two of ham and warm up some sweet potatoes, which you might have in your freezer, you'll find someone turning on a Dixieland jazz record.

3 tablespoons bacon fat	1 pint okra, canned or frozen
½ cup chopped onion (fresh or frozen)	2 teaspoons brown sugar
½ cup chopped green pepper (fresh or frozen)	1 teaspoon lemon juice
1 clove garlic, minced	1 bay leaf
1 pint canned tomatoes (coarsely chopped)	⅛ teaspoon powdered thyme Salt and pepper

Heat the fat in a saucepan and sauté the onion and pepper and garlic for 2 minutes. Add the tomatoes with the juice and bring to a boil. Drain the okra if using the canned variety. The frozen okra can be added frozen or partially thawed. Add the sugar, lemon juice and bay leaf. Bring to a boil. Simmer uncovered for 20 minutes. Season to taste with salt and pepper.

Remove the bay leaf and serve the gumbo in side dishes.

Serves 4 persons.

Peas

Select fresh green garden-picked pea pods which are well and uniformly filled. The pods should look crisp and unwrinkled; the peas within the pods green and firm. Two to 4 pounds of peas in the pod will yield 1 pint of canned or frozen.

Shell and wash the peas. Discard immature or tough peas.

CANNING

Cold Pack: Pack peas to within 1 inch of top; do not shake or press down. Add ½ teaspoon of salt if desired. Add boiling water, leaving 1½ inches of space at top of jar. Adjust lids and closures. Process in pressure saucepan at 10 pounds pressure for 60 minutes. Allow 40 minutes in a standard pressure canner.

Hot Pack: Cover the prepared peas with boiling water. Bring to a boil. Pack hot peas loosely to within ¼ inch of top, adding ½ teaspoon of salt if desired. Add the boiling liquid in which they were scalded to within 1 inch of top of jar.

Process pints in pressure saucepan at 10 pounds pressure for 60 minutes, 40 minutes in a standard pressure canner.

FREEZING

Shell and wash peas. Heat in boiling water 1½ minutes. Drain and plunge into icy water. Drain.

Pack peas into containers, leaving ½ inch head space. Seal, label and freeze.

French Green Peas

This recipe originally devised for fresh peas by some ingenious French-man adapts itself very well to home-frozen peas.

1   pint frozen peas
    The heart of a Boston
    or garden lettuce
3   tablespoons butter
    or margarine
    Several sprigs fresh
    parsley

10 scallions (green
    onions)
½   teaspoon salt
1   teaspoon sugar
1   egg yolk, slightly beaten

In an enamel-lined or glass saucepan, combine the peas, the lettuce heart, 1½ tablespoons of the butter or margarine, the parsley, the trimmed white bulbs of the scallions, the salt and sugar. Cover and let stand at room temperature for 45 minutes. Remove cover.

Using the French method, cover the saucepan with a shallow dish or pie plate containing a quarter cup of water. Cook gently for 30 minutes.

Drain off the liquid into a small saucepan. Remove the parsley and cut the lettuce into 2 or 3 serving pieces. Place them in a heated vegetable dish and pour the onions and peas over them.

Beat the egg yolk into the hot vegetable juice and whisk in the remaining butter or margarine over moderate heat just until the butter melts. Do not boil. Taste for seasoning. Pour over the peas and serve.

Serves 2 or 3 persons.

Peas—Black-eyed

Black-eyed peas are also known as field peas, cowpeas and black-eyed beans. They are suitable for both canning and freezing. Select well-filled flexible pods with tender seeds. Three pounds in the pod will produce 1 pint when processed.

Shell the peas, discarding any seeds that are hard. Wash.

CANNING

Cold Pack: Pack raw black-eyed peas to within 1½ inches of top of pint jars; do not shake or press down. Add ½ teaspoon salt if desired. Cover with boiling water or canning bouillon, leaving ½ inch space at top of jars. Adjust the lids and closures. Process in pressure saucepan at 10 pounds pressure for 55 minutes. Allow 35 minutes in standard pressure canner.

Hot Pack: Cover the peas with boiling water and bring to a rolling boil. Drain.

Pack hot peas to within 1¼ inches of top of jars without shaking or pressing down. Add ½ teaspoon salt if desired. Cover with boiling water or canning bouillon, leaving ½ inch space at top of jar. Adjust lids and closures. Process in pressure saucepan at 10 pounds' pressure for 55 minutes. Allow 35 minutes for standard pressure canner.

FREEZING

Prepare peas as above. Heat in boiling water for 2 minutes. Plunge into icy water to cool and drain. Pack into freezing containers, leaving ½ inch head space. Seal, label and freeze.

Louisiana Black-eyed Peas en Casserole

¾-1 pound Canadian bacon	1 pint black-eyed peas
1 bay leaf	(canned or frozen)
2 cloves	1 cup raw rice
1 onion, sliced	1 pint canned tomatoes
	Salt and Tabasco

Put the bacon in a kettle. Cover with water by 1 inch. Add the bay leaf, cloves and onion. Bring to a boil and simmer for 1 hour.

Add the peas. Cover and cook 30 minutes, making sure there is enough water to cover the peas.

Add the rice and cook 20 minutes uncovered.

Add the tomatoes and continue to cook until the mixture is fairly thick. Season with salt if necessary and add the Tabasco to taste. Remember it is powerful stuff.

Remove the bacon, bay leaf and the cloves (if you can find them) from the dish.

Cut the bacon into serving pieces. Arrange the vegetables in a deep platter and lay the bacon on top. Serve very hot.

Serves 4 to 6 persons.

Peas–Chinese Snow Peas

Chinese snow peas have gained great popularity in recent years outside the Chinese community. They can be grown abundantly wherever snap beans are grown, and they have an excellent flavor. We do not recommend them for canning, but freezing them is quick and easy. In order to have the snow peas tender, it is very important that the edible pods are picked when they are only about 3 inches long and the peas barely formed.

FREEZING

Scald the pods 1 minute in boiling water. Drain and plunge into cold water. Drain and dry on paper toweling.

Package and freeze.

Chinese Snow Peas and Beef

The remarkable thing about this recipe is how little beef goes into a dish for four people. Ask the butcher to cut off 4 ounces of sirloin tip or eye of the round beef in very thin slices. We usually buy the rest of the roast for future use, but for this recipe 4 ounces will be all you need.

1	pint frozen Chinese snow peas	2	teaspoons sherry
4	ounces sirloin tip or eye of the round beef, sliced thin	1	tablespoon soy sauce
		1	teaspoon sugar
		1	teaspoon salt
1	teaspoon cornstarch	½	cup sliced canned water chestnuts
1	teaspoon water	3	tablespoons oil

Thaw the peas just until you can separate them.

Place the beef in a bowl. Mix the cornstarch and water with the sherry, soy sauce, sugar and salt and mix it with the beef.

Drain and dry the chestnuts. Slice them very thin.

Heat 2 tablespoons of the oil in a wok, skillet or electric frying pan. Sauté the chestnuts, stirring until lightly browned. Remove from the skillet with a slotted spoon.

Add the remaining tablespoon of oil to the skillet and add the beef, tossing it with two forks for 30 seconds.

Add the peas and chestnuts and cook for 2 minutes.

Serve with cooked brown rice.

Serves 3 or 4 persons.

Peppers

Peppers are easy to grow, easy to can and easier still to freeze. We advise both canning and freezing partly because of storage space. If you can the peppers, you will be using them in cooked dishes; those you freeze you will want for sautéing or for salads. If you do both you will have the best of all possible pepper worlds. One-half pound of peppers (2 or 3) will yield a pint of canned peppers.

CANNING

Cut out the stems and cores of the pepper. Cut them in half and remove the seeds and membranes. Leave the peppers in halves, or cut them into smaller pieces according to your plans for them. Halves are excellent for stuffing and can be more conveniently packed than whole peppers. If you like an attractive combination, combine the green peppers with the red ones, which are the same vegetable—just riper. They can be canned in the same manner.

Parboil the peppers for 3 minutes in vigorously boiling water.

Drain and pack into hot, clean jars, leaving 1 inch head room.

Add 1 tablespoon of white vinegar and ½ teaspoon of canning salt.

Add just enough boiling water to cover.

Adjust the lids and closures. Process 55 minutes in the pressure saucepan (35 minutes in a standard pressure canner).

FREEZING

Peppers (green or red) do not have to be blanched before freezing. Dice them (see Frozen Standbys) or cut them in strips, in circles or in decorative shapes, after you have cored and removed the membranes and seeds. Pack them in small freezing containers, leaving no head room.

Seal, label and freeze.

Italian Chicken and Green Peppers

This will become a family favorite because it can be made in advance and reheated or put together very quickly, provided you have peppers in your canning closet or in your freezer.

1 chicken (2¾ to 3 pounds)	1 large clove garlic, peeled
½ cup flour	and minced (optional)
1 teaspoon salt	2 pints canned or frozen
1 tablespoon butter	pepper quarters
or margarine	½ pint canned tomatoes
2 tablespoons vegetable oil	½ teaspoon dried rosemary
4 tablespoons chopped onion	Salt and pepper

Put the chicken, flour and salt in a paper bag and shake well.

Heat the butter or margarine and oil in a skillet. Sauté the onion and garlic over moderate heat without browning. As soon as the onion is soft, remove it with a slotted spoon, leaving the fat in the pan. Reserve the onion.

Turn up the heat under the skillet and brown the chicken on all sides.

Place the dark meat on the bottom of a deep baking-serving dish. Cover with 1 pint of drained peppers, half the tomatoes and half the onions. Put the chicken breasts on top and cover with the remaining peppers, onions and tomatoes. Sprinkle with salt, pepper and rosemary. Cover and bake on the next-to-bottom shelf of the oven for 20 minutes at 375 degrees F. Remove the cover and bake 10 minutes longer. Serve with plenty of Italian bread and Chianti; it takes a hearty wine to meet the flavor of this dish.

Serves 4 to 6 persons.

Pimientos

Pimientos are a special type of sweet red pepper grown in southern climes. They can be stuffed like green peppers or used as a garnish for soups, salads and other culinary preparations. They are also a delicious vegetable when cooked with onion and tomatoes. Pimientos can be canned in a pressure cooker or frozen.

CANNING

Wash the pimientos well. Cut in half, removing the stem, seeds and membranes. Place the halves under a broiler or in a preheated 400-degree oven, cut side down. When the skins are charred, place the pimientos in icy cold water. Usually the skins will slip off quite easily. Drain the peppers and flatten them with the palm of your hand.

Pack the peppers into 4-ounce or 8-ounce clean, hot jars without using any water, leaving ½ inch head room. Add ⅛ teaspoon of salt and

1 teaspoon of white vinegar to the 4-ounce jars; ½ teaspoon salt and ½ tablespoon of vinegar to the 8-ounce size.

Put on the lids and closures.

Process at 10 pounds' pressure for 40 minutes in a pressure saucepan or 20 minutes in a standard pressure canner.

FREEZING

Prepare the pimientos as for canning.

Pack in 4-ounce or 8-ounce containers, leaving ½ inch head room.

Seal, label and freeze.

Pimiento and Tomato Omelet

This omelet, reminiscent of Tunisian cooking, makes a lovely lunch or brunch dish. The filling may be made in advance and reheated or kept warm, the eggs can be prepared also, so that the last-minute cooking will be a matter of seconds. In fact, if your guest list is large, triple or quadruple the filling and make individual omelets on demand in a 5-inch skillet.

FILLING:

2	tablespoons olive oil	¼	teaspoon sugar
½	cup finely chopped onions (fresh or frozen)	¾	teaspoon salt
		¼	teaspoon pepper
1	8-ounce can pimientos (canned or frozen)		
			OMELET:
1	pint canned tomatoes	6	eggs
1	teaspoon fresh chopped basil or ¼ teaspoon dried basil	4	tablespoons butter or margarine
		½	teaspoon salt
		⅛	teaspoon white pepper

Filling: Heat the olive oil in a saucepan and sauté the onions just until tender. Add the pimientos (thawed, if frozen) cut in wide strips, the tomatoes, basil, sugar, salt and pepper. Cook over moderate heat until the mixture is fairly thick. Season to taste.

Omelet: Break the eggs into a bowl and whisk with a fork or whip until the yolks and whites are blended. Cut 3 tablespoons of the butter or margarine into the eggs. Add the salt and pepper.

Heat a 10-inch omelet pan and, when it is quite hot, add the remaining butter or margarine. Swirl the butter around in the pan to coat the entire surface. Add the egg mixture and cook without stirring until the underside has set. Lift the edges with a fork or small spatula to let the uncooked egg seep through. When the omelet is almost cooked, with just a little liquid left on top, remove from the heat. Put the filling on one-half of the omelet and flip the other side over with the help of a spatula or, if you are feeling professional, give a quick jerk to the pan, which will accomplish the flipping process.

Slip the omelet onto a warm (not hot) serving platter, or serve directly from the omelet pan.

Serve with buttered and toasted whole wheat Syrian bread.

Serves 3 or 4 persons.

Spinach (and Other Greens)

Freshly picked tender spinach and other greens may be canned or frozen. Select young, tender leaves. Two to 6 pounds of greens will yield 2 pints of processed food.

CANNING

Pick over and wash thoroughly in several waters, cutting out tough stems. Place about 2 to 3 pounds of greens in a cheesecloth bag and steam until well wilted—about 10 minutes.

Pack hot spinach (or greens) *loosely* to within ½ inch of top. Add ¼ teaspoon of salt if desired. Cover with boiling water or canning bouillon, leaving ½ inch of head space. Run a nonmetal rod around the jar to release any air bubbles.

Adjust the jar lids.

Process in pressure saucepan 10 pounds pressure for 1 hour and 30 minutes (70 minutes in standard pressure canner).

Remove the jars and set on a rack or towel to cool, leaving plenty of air space between jars.

Label and store.

FREEZING

Wash young, tender leaves well, removing the tough stems. Leaves of chard may be cut into pieces if desired.

Heat the greens in boiling water for 2 minutes. Plunge into cold or iced water and drain.

Pack into containers, leaving ½ inch head space.

Seal and freeze.

Spinach and Bacon Soufflé

1 pint frozen chopped spinach	½ cup milk
2 slices bacon	3 egg yolks, beaten
4 tablespoons chopped onions	⅛ teaspoon nutmeg
1 clove garlic, minced	Salt and pepper
3 tablespoons butter or margarine	3 egg whites
3 tablespoons unbleached or whole wheat pastry flour	

Butter a soufflé or straight-sided baking dish.

Bring the spinach to a boil with 2 tablespoons of water. Break up the frozen block with a fork for even cooking. Boil 3 minutes. Drain in a colander, pressing out all the liquid possible with the back of a spoon. Save the liquid.

Cook the bacon in a small skillet over moderate heat until crisp.

Dry the bacon on paper toweling and pour off all but 1 tablespoon of the fat. Sauté the onion and garlic in the fat just until tender. Set aside.

Preheat the oven to 350 degrees F.

Heat the butter or margarine in a small saucepan. Whisk in the flour, and, when it is well blended, add ½ cup of spinach broth and ½ cup of milk. Whisk until smooth and thick. Add the drained spinach, crumbled bacon and onion, and, when they are well mixed, gradually add the beaten egg yolks, whisking vigorously. Cook 1 minute, still whisking. Remove from the heat. Season to taste with nutmeg, salt and pepper.

Beat the egg whites stiff. Fold them carefully into the spinach mixture. Pour into the prepared dish and bake 35 to 40 minutes, depending on how dry you like soufflés.

Serve immediately.

Note: If you want to prepare the soufflé in advance, do everything up to beating the egg whites. Be sure that your spinach mixture is at room temperature when folding in the egg whites.

Squash—Summer Squash

Summer squash is a bland vegetable that does not improve in either flavor or texture when canned. However, when it is combined with other vegetables, it can be a very satisfactory almost-ready-to-eat meal.

Canned Summer Squash Mix

4 cups prepared summer squash

4 cups prepared tomatoes (medium to small)

½ cup diced celery

Choose small tender squash. Wash well and cut in ½-inch slices.

Dice the celery.

Place the vegetables in a steaming basket. Lower it into enough briskly boiling water to cover. Boil 3 minutes. Retrieve and shake as dry as possible. Spread the vegetables out on paper toweling and pat dry with more toweling.

Using the same steamer, lower well-washed tomatoes into the same liquid for 30 seconds, doing 4 or 5 tomatoes at a time. Cool by placing in cold water and then peel off the skins. Halve and gently squeeze out as many of the seeds as possible. Place in a colander or on a rack over a pan to drain. Let the cooking liquid boil down.

Place a layer of the squash/celery mixture in the bottoms of 2 hot, clean pint jars. Cover with a layer of tomato halves. Alternate the layers until the jars are tightly filled up to within 1 inch of the top. Add ½ teaspoon of canning salt and just enough of the cooking liquid to cover.

Adjust the lids and closures.

Process at 10 pounds pressure in a pressure saucepan for 45 minutes. Allow 25 minutes for a standard pressure canner.

Yields 2 pints.

Summer Squash and Tomato Casserole

2 tablespoons butter or margarine	1 pint Summer Squash Mix (well drained)
4 tablespoons chopped onion (fresh or frozen)	1 cup seasoned Italian croutons
4 tablespoons chopped peppers (fresh or frozen)	Garlic salt and pepper
	½ cup grated Parmesan cheese

Preheat the oven to 350 degrees F.

Heat 1 tablespoon of the butter or margarine in a small skillet, and sauté the onions and peppers just until tender. Remove from the heat.

Butter a small oven-serving casserole. Spread the bottom with ⅓ cup of the croutons. Cover with half the Summer Squash Mix and sprinkle with half the onion and pepper mix. Sprinkle with garlic salt and white pepper. Repeat the process.

Heat the remaining butter in the same skillet and sauté the remaining croutons until golden brown. Spread the croutons over the top of the casserole. Sprinkle with Parmesan cheese.

Bake 20 minutes.

Serves 2 to 4 persons.

Squash—Winter Squash

Winter squash may be canned, but we prefer to freeze it. Since it is in all probability to be used either for pies or as a mashed vegetable, we prefer to can or freeze it pureed rather than cut in cubes.

For small kitchens, choose the Butternut, Turban or small Green Delicious. Except for the Butternut, use only squash that are hard-shelled and mature.

Cut the squash in half and remove the seeds and fibers. The squash can then be cut in small pieces and peeled and steamed, or left with the skin on and baked cut side down on a trivet rack over a pan of hot water until tender. The length of cooking time will vary between 15 to 40 minutes.

Put the cooked squash through a food mill or spin in a food processor.

CANNING

Reheat the squash over low heat or in a double boiler.

Pack very hot into hot, clean pint and ½-pint jars.

Process 1¼ hours in a pressure saucepan (55 minutes in a standard pressure canner).

FREEZING

Prepare the squash as above. Cool thoroughly, stirring occasionally. Pack into pint and ½-pint freezer containers, leaving ½ inch head space. Seal, label and freeze.

Sherry Squash Pie

1 baked pie shell (bought or homemade)	½ teaspoon powdered ginger
1 pint plus ½ pint frozen or canned squash	1 teaspoon powdered cinnamon
12 ounces evaporated milk	3 large eggs, slightly beaten with
¾ cup honey or maple syrup	4 tablespoons sherry
¼ teaspoon cloves	Candied ginger
	¼ pint heavy cream, whipped

Make or buy the pie shell.

Heat the squash in the covered top of a double boiler until all excess moisture has disappeared.

Combine the milk, honey or maple syrup and the spices with the eggs and sherry in a bowl and blend well.

Pour the milk mixture gradually into the squash, stirring constantly. Cook 5 minutes, stirring frequently.

Pour the mixture into the pie shell, smoothing the top with a spatula.

At serving time decorate the center with candied ginger and circle the edge with whipped cream.

Sweet Potatoes

Sweet potatoes take so much time and fuel energy to can that we prefer to have just a couple of pints in the freezer ready for serving. Sweet potatoes vary in size greatly, but 4 medium size should yield 2 pints of prepared potatoes. With your pressure saucepan this can be done in very short order.

FREEZING

Scrub the potatoes very thoroughly but do not peel. Place on a rack in the pressure saucepan. Add 1½ cups of water. Adjust the cover and pressure regulator. Pressure cook for 10 minutes. Place the pan in cold water for quick cooling. Do not remove the regulator until the steam no longer escapes. Remove the cover and take out the potatoes.

Hold each potato with a fork and remove the skin with a sharp knife.

Mash immediately and season with 4 tablespoons of butter or margarine, 4 tablespoons of orange juice and 1 tablespoon of lemon juice. Season to taste with salt and pepper.

Pack into pint containers, leaving ½ inch head space. Seal, label and freeze.

Before serving reheat in a double boiler. Taste for seasoning and add a dash of nutmeg.

Swiss Chard

Swiss chard is one of the most prolific of vegetables and one that a gardener friend is always anxious to give away. We don't recommend canning it, although we will give the recipe for those who don't own a freezer. Swiss chard will can very well, but it takes 1 hour and 30 minutes to cook it in a pressure saucepan (70 minutes in a standard pressure cooker), which seems excessive from the point of view of energy usage. Freezing chard is a quick process.

Two pounds of Swiss chard will yield approximately 1 pound of greens and ¾ pound of trimmed stalks. This will yield 1 pint of frozen greens and ½ pint of blanched and frozen stalks.

CANNING

Wash the chard thoroughly, removing the stems and thick ribs. Save the stems. Put 1 inch of boiling water in a kettle. Add 1 pound of greens. Cook over high heat for 4 to 6 minutes, turning with a fork to hasten the wilting process.

Cut the greens coarsely with a knife and spoon them into hot pint jars. Add boiling water or canning bouillon and ½ teaspoon of canning salt. Leave 1 inch of head space.

Adjust caps and closures and process 1 hour and 30 minutes in a pressure saucepan or 70 minutes in a standard pressure canner at 10 pounds pressure.

Chard Stems: Wash the stems and trim them evenly 1 inch shorter than the container. Fill pint jars, leaving 1 inch head space. Adjust lids and closures. Process 45 minutes at 10 pounds pressure in a pressure saucepan.

FREEZING

Prepare the chard as above. Blanch the well-washed greens for 2 minutes in 3 inches of water. Do not blanch more than 1 pound at a time. Drain thoroughly and pat dry with paper toweling. Pack in pint boxes, leaving ½ inch head space. Seal, label and freeze.

Stems: Scald the stems 1½ minutes. Drain well. The stalks may be left whole for braising or may be chopped. Pack into ½-pint containers, leaving ¼ inch head room. Seal, label and freeze.

Swiss Chard Casserole

This can be prepared in advance.

1 pint frozen or canned Swiss chard	1 pint Swiss chard stems frozen, partially thawed, or canned
3½ tablespoons butter or margarine	½ cup chopped onion
2 tablespoons flour	½ cup Italian seasoned bread crumbs
1 cup light cream Salt, pepper and ⅛ teaspoon nutmeg	½ cup Parmesan cheese

Cook the canned or frozen chard with 2 tablespoons of water for 10 minutes. When cooking the frozen variety, break it up with a fork to insure even cooking.

Drain the cooked chard and place it in a blender with 2 tablespoons of butter or margarine, the flour, cream, salt, pepper and nutmeg. Blend until smooth. (If you do not have a blender, chop the chard quite fine and mix it with 1 cup of white sauce made with the same amounts of butter, flour and cream.)

Pour the mixture into a buttered quart-size oven-serving dish.

In a small skillet melt 1 tablespoon of butter or margarine. Sauté the chard stems, chopped, and the onion until tender. Add the bread crumbs and continue to cook until the crumbs are well blended. Remove from the heat and stir in the cheese. Spread the mixture over the creamed chard and dot with the remaining butter.

Before serving, bake 20 minutes at 350 degrees F.

Tomatoes

Tomatoes are one of the most popular vegetables in the American market. In recent years there has been much discussion about whether the newer species are totally safe from botulism when canned by the boiling water bath method. The fact is that their hybridization has produced sweeter and meatier varieties which, while delicious when eaten raw, can no longer be considered an acid fruit. Certain types of tomatoes, if canned when ripe but not overripe, are still considered safe for canning by the traditional method. But to be absolutely sure, we recommend that you check with your local Extension Service for the type of tomato that is safe, or follow the advice of the USDA Extension Service and add a little vinegar or citric acid to each jar. This will not affect the flavor. Freezing tomatoes is perfectly possible, but for best results in small quarters we recommend canning. A pint of canned tomatoes can be the basis of all sorts of good recipes. Whether you are canning by boiling water bath or pressure saucepan, plan on 4 pint jars at a time. This will mean approximately 6 pounds or about 2 dozen medium-size tomatoes.

CANNING

Cold Pack: Sort tomatoes of approximately the same size for easier packing. Wash well and dip a few at a time in a steaming basket into boiling water. Hold for 30 seconds. Transfer to very cold water. Hold for 30 seconds, then slip off the skins and drop the tomatoes into clean jars. Fill the jars to within ½ inch of the top. If the tomatoes are very juicy, pour off the excess juice into a bowl and press the tomatoes down gently, getting in as many as possible. Cut some of the tomatoes in halves or quarters to fill in any empty spaces. Add ½ teaspoon of salt and ½ teaspoon of sugar to each pint jar if desired. If you are not sure about the type of tomato, add ¼ teaspoon of citric acid or 1 tablespoon of white vinegar. Wipe the lip of the jar with a hot, damp towel. Adjust the lids.

Place the filled jars on a steaming rack in a kettle of hot (not boiling) water. There should be at least 1 inch of water over the tops of the jars. Bring to a boil and boil 35 minutes.

Remove and cool on a towel or rack. When jars are cold, remove the screw bands, check the seals, label and store in a dark closet.

Hot Pack: Wash the tomatoes. Put a few in a steamer basket and dip into a kettle of boiling water for 30 seconds. Remove and plunge into cold water. Slip off the skins and cut the tomatoes into quarters into a large saucepan. Repeat the process until all are prepared. Bring the tomatoes to a boil, stirring occasionally, very gently.

Pour the tomatoes into hot, clean jars to within ½ inch of the top. Add ½ teaspoon of salt and ½ teaspoon of sugar if desired. Add ¼ teaspoon of citric acid or 1 tablespoon of white vinegar if you are not absolutely sure of the acidity of the tomatoes.

Wipe the lips of the jars with a hot, damp towel, and adjust the lids.

Place in a steaming rack in boiling water to cover the jars by 1 inch. Cover and boil 15 minutes. Complete the process as above.

Pressure Canning: Prepare the tomatoes as though for cold pack.

Place the jars on a rack in a pressure saucepan containing 2 inches of boiling water. Process 35 minutes at 10 pounds pressure, or 15 minutes in a pressure canner.

Sicilian Tomato and Swiss Chard Soup

This is a delicious peasant soup that serves as a main dish for luncheon or supper. For added sustenance serve salami sandwiches made with warm, crusty Italian rolls, and glasses of hearty red wine.

1 medium onion, chopped	½ cup water
1 large clove garlic, minced	Salt and freshly ground
2 tablespoons olive oil	black pepper
1 pint canned tomatoes	Parmesan cheese, freshly
1 pint canned or frozen	grated
Swiss chard	

Sauté the onion and garlic in oil for 1 minute. Add the tomatoes and Swiss chard with their liquid. Add the water.

Cover and simmer 15 minutes. Season to taste with salt and pepper. Serve in soup plates liberally sprinkled with Parmesan cheese.

Serves 4 persons.

Tomato Shrimp Casserole

This is a quick and easy meal, especially if you happen to have 2 cups of leftover brown or white cooked rice.

1 medium onion, chopped	1 pint cooked and shelled
1 medium green pepper, chopped	shrimp (fresh, frozen,
4 tablespoons butter or	canned)
margarine	2 cups cooked brown or
1 pint canned tomatoes,	white rice
undrained	3 hard-cooked eggs
½ teaspoon dried basil	½ cup finely chopped parsley
2-3 drops Tabasco	Salt and black pepper

Prepare the vegetables and sauté them in the butter or margarine until tender.

Add the tomatoes, basil and Tabasco and simmer 5 minutes. Season to taste with salt, add the shrimp and simmer 10 minutes. Do not boil.

Butter a small casserole and cover the bottom with half the rice. Cover with half the shrimp-tomato mixture. Repeat the process.

Cover and bake 20 minutes at 350 degrees F.

Meanwhile, cook the eggs 12 minutes. Peel and chop them very fine. Mix with the parsley.

Just before serving the casserole, sprinkle the surface with the egg and parsley mixture and with freshly ground black pepper.

Tomato Juice

Tomato juice has to be very special to deserve storage room on either the shelf or in the freezer of a small home. This one is just that special and can be served very cold as an aperitif or hot as bouillon. For a spicier taste, add a drop or two of Tabasco sauce just before serving.

1½ cups water	2 stalks celery with leaves, coarsely chopped
2 fresh basil leaves or	
1 teaspoon dried basil	2 tablespoons chopped green pepper
1 bay leaf	
1 sprig thyme or	2 dozen medium-size ripe tomatoes
⅛ teaspoon powdered thyme	
6 peppercorns	2 teaspoons salt
6 sprigs parsley	¼ teaspoon white pepper
	½ teaspoon sugar

Put the water in a small saucepan.

Put the basil leaves, bay leaf, thyme, peppercorns and parsley in a stainless steel or enamel tea ball and drop in the water. Bring to a rapid boil and simmer, partially covered, while preparing the tomatoes.

Wash the tomatoes well, removing the stem ends. Cut into quarters into an enamel-lined or stainless steel pan. Do not use iron.

Remove the tea ball and pour contents of the saucepan into the tomatoes. Bring to a simmer and cook without boiling for 10 minutes.

Force the tomatoes through a food mill or coarse strainer and then through a fine strainer. Season with salt, pepper and sugar.

CANNING

Reheat the juice to the boiling point and pour into clean, hot jars, leaving ½ inch head room. Adjust the lids and closures.

Place the jars in a rack in a boiling water bath canner with hot water, covering the jars by at least an inch. Bring to a boil and process for 15 minutes. Remove the jars to a damp towel or rack and let them cool with air space in between. Label and store in a dark closet.

FREEZING

Prepare the juice as above. Cool and pour into plastic or glass freezer containers, leaving 1½ inches of head space. Seal, label and freeze.

Tomato Sauces

No self-respecting kitchen will be without a tomato sauce on hand because tomato sauce can be the basis of many a good dish that can be prepared in minutes. We prefer to can the vegetable-based sauce and freeze the meat-based—but that is only a personal preference. Either can be frozen.

Tomato Sauce I (Meatless)

7 cups prepared tomatoes	1 large clove garlic, minced
2 tablespoons olive oil	1 teaspoon oregano
2 tablespoons butter or margarine	2 basil leaves, snipped
	1 teaspoon salt
¾ cup chopped onion	½ teaspoon sugar
½ cup chopped green peppers	

Wash the tomatoes and dip 4 or 5 at a time in boiling water for 30 seconds, using a steaming basket for easy retrieval. Dip in cold water for 30 seconds. Slip off the skins and remove the stem ends. Cut into quarters into a measuring cup and then into a bowl. When you have 7 cups, prepare the rest of the sauce.

Heat the oil and butter or margarine. Stir in the onions, peppers and garlic. Cook until the onion is soft.

Add the tomatoes, oregano, basil leaves, salt and sugar. Stir until the mixture boils. Reduce the heat and simmer 15 minutes or until the mixture is fairly thick.

CANNING

Pour the hot tomato sauce into hot, clean jars, leaving ½ inch head room. Adjust the lids and closures. Place on a rack in a pressure saucepan and process 30 minutes at 10 pounds pressure (10 minutes in a standard pressure canner). Remove from the heat and do not open the canner until the pressure has returned to zero.

Remove the jars to a damp towel or rack and let cool with air space between the jars. When they are cooled, label and store in a dark place.

FREEZING

Make the sauce as above. Cool and chill before packing into plastic freezer containers or glass jars, leaving 1 inch head room. Seal, label and freeze.

Tomato Sauce II (With Meat)

6 *cups prepared tomatoes*	½ *cup red wine*
(approximately 16 tomatoes)	1 *bay leaf*
2 *cups chopped onion*	2 *basil leaves*
1 *clove garlic, minced*	6 *sprigs parsley*
½ *large green pepper, chopped*	⅛ *teaspoon powdered thyme*
1 *small carrot, chopped*	1½ *teaspoons salt*
4 *tablespoons butter or*	¼ *teaspoon pepper*
margarine	1 *pound ground veal or beef*
2 *tablespoons olive oil*	

Wash the tomatoes. Dip them for 30 seconds in boiling water. Plunge into cold water and remove the skins. Cut the tomatoes in half and gently squeeze out the seeds. The Italian plum tomatoes are the best for this use, but the ordinary varieties are perfectly satisfactory.

Prepare the vegetables.

Heat 2 tablespoons of butter or margarine and 2 tablespoons of oil in a large skillet (not iron). Sauté the vegetables for 3 minutes, stirring with a wooden spoon. Add the tomatoes and the wine. Tie the bay leaf, basil and parsley into a little bouquet or place them in a stainless steel or enamel tea ball. Add them and the powdered thyme to the tomatoes along with salt, pepper and sugar. Bring to a boil, stirring. Reduce the heat and simmer 30 minutes.

Heat the remaining butter in a small skillet. Cook the meat until all the red color has disappeared. Set aside.

Remove the herbs from the tomato mixture. Force the sauce through a food mill or strainer or spin briefly in a blender or food processor, doing no more than 2 cups at a time.

Combine the resulting sauce with the cooked meat. Cover and simmer 15 minutes. Remove from the heat, taste for seasoning and add ½ teaspoon of sugar if the sauce seems a little acid. Cool and then chill.

Pack in freezer containers, leaving 1 inch of head room.

Seal, label and freeze.

Tomato Paste

Making tomato paste had always seemed like a very long process until a lady on the coast of Maine gave us her secret. If you just do 2 or 3 pounds you will get 2 ½-pint jars and a lot of satisfaction out of it. We usually can the paste; after a jar is opened, it can be kept in the freezer for further use.

Wash the tomatoes thoroughly, removing the stem end. Italian plum tomatoes are the best, but any variety will do.

Cut the tomatoes coarsely into a kettle. Bring to a boil and simmer 3 minutes.

Drain in a colander placed over a bowl for about 2 hours or until all the liquid is gone. Save the liquid for tomato juice, soup or sauces.

Force the dry pulp through a food mill, removing the skin and the seeds. Put the sieved pulp back on the stove in a heavy enamel-lined saucepan. Cook until thick. Season just with ¼ teaspoon of salt per ½ pint. Adding other spices limits its use to specific dishes.

CANNING

Pour hot tomato paste into clean, hot jars, filling within ¼ inch of the top. Adjust lids and closures. Place on a rack in boiling water to cover by 1 inch and process 30 minutes.

Set jars well apart on rack or towel to cool, then label and store.

Hurry-up Tomato Sauce

If the tomato sauces on the shelf or in the freezer are exhausted and you still have some tomato paste and tomatoes in reserve, you can produce a good sauce in very little time.

1 medium onion, shredded	1 bay leaf
1 carrot, shredded	½ teaspoon oregano
1 clove garlic, minced	¼ teaspoon sugar
2 tablespoons olive oil	1 can (10½ ounces) beef
1 pint canned tomatoes	bouillon
4 tablespoons canned	4 ounces Italian salami, diced
tomato paste	Salt and black pepper
½ cup red wine	

Shred the onion and well-washed carrot on a cheese grater or spin in a food processor. Sauté the vegetables and the minced garlic in the oil for 2 minutes. Add the tomatoes and the tomato paste blended with the wine. Bring to a boil. Add the bay leaf and the oregano, the sugar and the beef bouillon. Bring again to a boil and boil hard for 3 minutes. Reduce the heat and cook 15 minutes longer. Remove the bay leaf and add the diced salami. Cook 5 minutes longer. Season to taste with salt and pepper.

Serve with the pasta of your choice.

Serves 4 to 6 persons.

Zucchini

Zucchini can be canned or frozen. Like its close cousin, summer squash, it is bland and needs some spicing up. Mixed with tomato sauce, it makes a great addition to baked Lasagne. Slightly less caloric is Zucchini Suzanna.

FREEZING

Blanch the cut zucchini in boiling water for 3 minutes. Drain and plunge into icy water. Do not blanch more than about 1 pound at a time.

After draining, spread the zucchini on paper toweling. Pat dry and then let air dry for 1 or 2 hours. Pack in pint containers, leaving ½ inch head space. Seal, label and freeze.

CANNING

Select about 6 pounds of small, firm zucchini. Wash them very thoroughly and cut in ½-inch slices. Halve or quarter the larger pieces.

Cold Pack: Pack the slices into clean jars. Add ½ teaspoon of canning salt, if desired. Cover with boiling water, leaving 1 inch head space. Adjust the lids and closures. Process at 10 pounds pressure in a pressure saucepan for 45 minutes. Allow 25 minutes if using a standard pressure canner.

Hot Pack: Put the cut zucchini in boiling water to cover. Bring back to the boiling point. Drain, reserving the liquid. Place the squash rather loosely in hot, clean jars, adding ½ teaspoon salt if desired. Cover with the boiling liquid or with canning bouillon, leaving ½ inch of head space. Adjust the lids and closures. Process in a pressure saucepan at 10 pounds pressure for 50 minutes. (Allow 30 minutes if using the standard pressure canner.)

Zucchini Suzanna

2 pints zucchini	3 cups coarse, fresh
1 cup chicken broth	bread crumbs
4 tablespoons tomato paste	2 cups grated Cheddar cheese
Salt and pepper	2 tablespoons butter

Drain (or thaw) the zucchini. Pat dry.

Mix the broth with the tomato paste and stir into the zucchini.

Oil a rectangular oven-serving dish. Spread half the zucchini in the dish. Sprinkle with salt and pepper. Cover with half the bread crumbs and sprinkle with half the cheese. Repeat the process. Dot the surface with the butter and bake 30 minutes at 350 degrees F.

Serves 6 to 8 persons.

Canning and Freezing Fruits

Canning and freezing fruits in small quarters is just as tempting as putting up vegetables. Desserts are often the biggest headache a meal planner has and when there is applesauce or peaches in the canning cupboard, or raspberries and strawberries in the freezer, there is very little to worry about. Again, family preference should be the chief guide.

Because many of us are interested in cutting down on sugar intake, we will give you the standard procedures of canning and freezing and then tell you our method of canning with fruit juices.

Most fruit can be canned or frozen for future use. In some cases one method is better than another, which we will indicate. Canned fruits are processed easily in a boiling water bath. For uniformity and for reassurance that your canning will be a success, we recommend the pint jars with self-sealing lids and screw-on bands. Limit yourself to 4 jars at a time and the process will be done in very short time. Freezing fruits is similarly uncomplicated. Follow directions for preparing the fruit and pack in scrupulously clean containers.

The quicker the transfer from orchard or bush to the jar or freezing container, the better the product. Don't waste your time and effort on inferior fruit. Choose firm, ripe fruit—but not overripe. We will give you an indication of how much you should buy. In no time at all you will have a treasure house of varied fruits on your storage shelves.

Apples

Apples can be stored without canning or freezing for a long time provided you have the proper storage space. Lacking that, it is good to put some apples in various forms in both the freezer and on the canning shelf. Our system is to process 8 or 9 pounds at a time and when the results of that effort are consumed we repeat the process with a later crop of apples. This amount will give you 2 pints of applesauce and 48 ounces of apple-pie slices (canned or frozen) plus some apple juice for cooking, canning or drinking. Tart apples are especially good for processing, but for those who are averse to using any sugar at all we recommend the sweeter varieties. If you are using these, we recommend that ¼ teaspoon of vitamin C (ascorbic acid) be added to every pint of prepared fruit.

Applesauce

Wash 3 to 3 ½ pounds of apples very thoroughly. Quarter and core the apples, setting the cores aside for future use. Do not peel the apples. Place them in a saucepan with ½ cup of water, and bring to a boil and simmer for about 10 minutes, or until soft. Stir occasionally to prevent scorching. Force the sauce through a food mill or coarse strainer.

CANNING

Unsweetened: Reheat the sauce without adding any sugar. Pack hot into clean, hot jars, leaving ½ inch of head space. Insert a wooden or plastic knife to release any air bubbles. Put on the lids and closures.

Place the pints in boiling water with at least 1 inch of water over the tops. Bring to a boil and process for 10 minutes. Remove the jars from the water to a towel or rack, leaving air space between the jars. Label and store.

A little artificial sweetener and cinnamon may be added to the canned applesauce before serving if desired.

Sweetened: Reheat the applesauce and sweeten to taste with white sugar, brown sugar or honey. Add ⅛ teaspoon of cinnamon for each pint of applesauce. Pack and process as above.

FREEZING

Prepare the applesauce as if for canning. Pack in pint jars or plastic containers, leaving ½ inch of head room. Seal, label and freeze.

Unsweetened Apple Juice for Canning

While the applesauce is processing, cut up 2 pounds (6 or 7) of well-washed apples. Add to them the cores of the fruit used for the applesauce. Add 2 cups of water. Bring to a boil and simmer ½ hour. Drain into a bowl through a jelly bag or a colander lined with a double thickness of cheesecloth. Bottle and cap the juice and store in the refrigerator.

Apples for Pies and Tarts

If you have canned or frozen apples ready for making an apple pie or tart, you are never caught short for dessert. If you are not a pastry maker, look in the freezer section of your market or use the simple crumb crusts. When canning apple slices, we put them in 12-ounce jars. Two of these will make a man-size pie. One will make a delicate French tart. When freezing pie slices, we pack them in aluminum-foil pie plates. Then they are the proper size and shape to slip into a pie crust.

Buy 4 to 6 pounds of apples. Wash them well.

Prepare some anti-darkening solution by measuring 1 quart of water and 4 teaspoons of powdered ascorbic acid (vitamin C) and mixing well.

Prepare one of the following canning liquids in an enamel-lined saucepan: (a) 1½ cups of prepared unsweetened apple juice, or (b) ½ cup sugar with 1¼ cups of water, or (c) 4 tablespoons of sugar with 4 tablespoons of honey and 1 cup of water.

Peel and core the apples using a sharp knife or one of the many gadgets made for speeding up the process. Cut into thin slices and drop into the anti-darkening solution. When all the apples are prepared, bring the canning liquid of your choice to a boil.

Drain the apples and add them to the saucepan. Cover and bring to a boil. Cook 1 minute. Remove from the heat.

CANNING

Using a slotted spoon, fill the jars with the cooked fruit to within ¾ inch of the top. Add hot liquid to cover, leaving ½ inch head space. Put on the lids and closures. Process in a boiling water bath for 15 minutes. Remove the jars from the water to a towel or rack and cool with air space between the jars. Label and store.

FREEZING

Sweetened: Make a syrup by dissolving ½ cup of sugar in ½ cup of hot water. When it is thoroughly dissolved add ¾ cup of very cold water. Put ½ cup of the syrup into each freezing container. Add ¼ teaspoon of ascorbic acid (vitamin C) in powdered form.

Slice the peeled and cored apple quarters directly into the syrup. Press them down gently to fill the jars as full as possible. Add the remaining syrup to cover the fruit, leaving ½ inch head space. Seal, label and freeze.

Unsweetened: Add ½ teaspoon of liquid artificial sweetener and ½ teaspoon of ascorbic acid to 1½ cups of apple juice. Pack and freeze as above, using the apple juice instead of syrup.

French Apple Tart

This tart is all apple and makes a regal dessert. The shell can be made in a round or rectangular shape, or you can purchase a single unbaked pie shell.

1 single pie crust	Sugar to taste
1 pint applesauce	1 12-ounce jar apple slices
1 teaspoon vanilla extract	4 tablespoons apple jelly
1 tablespoon melted butter	French Cream
½ teaspoon cinnamon	

Preheat the oven to 400 degrees F. Line an 8-inch pie tin with pie pastry. Prick the bottom well.

Add the vanilla, butter and cinnamon to the applesauce and add sugar to taste if necessary. Spread the sauce in the shell. Drain the slices and place them decoratively all over the surface. Sprinkle very lightly with sugar. Bake 30 minutes. Place on a rack to cool.

If the slices have been packed in syrup, boil down the drained syrup quickly to the jelly stage or until it sheets off a metal spoon. Or heat 4 tablespoons of apple jelly. When the tart is cool, spoon the sauce over the surface. Serve with or without French Cream.

French Cream

French Cream is made by heating ½ pint of heavy cream with 2 tablespoons of buttermilk just to lukewarm. Pour into a canning jar. Cover loosely and let stand at room temperature for overnight. Cover tightly and shake for a moment. Refrigerate until ready for use. This is also delicious with canned apple slices, peaches, plums or nectarines.

Applesauce Oatmeal Cookies

1½ cups applesauce (lightly sweetened)
12 tablespoons (1½ sticks) butter or margarine
1 cup brown sugar

4 cups rolled oats
1 cup chopped walnuts
½ teaspoon salt
1 teaspoon vanilla extract

Boil the applesauce down until it measures 1 cup. It should be quite thick. Do not let it scorch. Set aside to cool.

Beat the butter or margarine with the brown sugar until light and creamy. Stir in the rolled oats, the walnuts, salt and vanilla. Fold in the cooled applesauce.

Preheat the oven to 375 degrees F.

Oil 2 baking sheets. Drop the cookies by teaspoonfuls onto the baking sheets, giving them a little room to spread. Bake 8 to 12 minutes. Remove from the oven and let cool 5 minutes before transferring to a rack.

Makes 4½ dozen cookies.

A Youngster's Apple Delight

The title does not prevent adults from enjoying this dessert. It was "invented" for some special young people and their enthusiasm gave the dessert its name.

1 quart canned or frozen (thawed) applesauce
½ teaspoon cinnamon
¼ teaspoon nutmeg
¼ teaspoon salt
1 tablespoon lemon juice
1½ cups graham cracker crumbs

¾ cup brown sugar
4 tablespoons melted butter or margarine
½ cup chopped pecans or walnuts
Cream or vanilla ice cream (optional)

Preheat the oven to 350 degrees F.

Combine the applesauce, spices, salt and lemon juice. Spread in a lightly buttered oven-serving dish.

In a small bowl, mix the crumbs, sugar, butter or margarine and nuts. Mix well and sprinkle over the top of the applesauce. Bake about 35 minutes or until the top is golden brown.

Serve warm (not hot) as is or embellish it with a little ice cream or cream.

Serves 6 to 8 persons.

Applesauce Cake

2½	cups unbleached flour	1	cup white sugar
1	teaspoon cinnamon	¾	cup brown sugar
½	teaspoon allspice	1	large egg
½	teaspoon cloves	1½	cups (12-ounce jar) applesauce
2	teaspoons soda		
¼	teaspoon salt	1	cup seedless raisins
½	cup boiling water	1	cup chopped walnuts
8	tablespoons (1 stick) butter or margarine (softened)	1	teaspoon vanilla or 2 tablespoons rum

Preheat the oven to 350 degrees F. Grease a 9-by-12-inch baking pan.

Mix the 6 dry ingredients in a bowl.

Bring the water to a boil.

Cream the butter or margarine with the sugars until smooth, using an electric beater if possible. Add the eggs and, when well blended, add the applesauce, beating until smooth.

Beat in half the dry ingredients and half the boiling water, and when the mixture is smooth add the remaining dry ingredients and water.

Stir in the raisins, nuts and vanilla or rum.

Pour the batter into the prepared pan and bake 1 hour.

Serve warm with a Cream Cheese Sauce or cold, plain or spread with Rum Butter Frosting.

Serves 6 to 8 persons.

Cream Cheese Sauce

Blend 1 small package (3½ ounces) cream cheese with ½ pint sour cream. Sweeten with 2 tablespoons of honey if desired. Serve at room temperature.

Rum Butter Frosting

4 *tablespoons butter*	1 *tablespoon rum*
1 *egg yolk*	1½-2 *cups confectioners' sugar*

Using an electric beater mix the butter, egg yolk and rum until smooth. Add 1½ cups of sugar and beat until smooth. Add just enough additional sugar to give a spreading consistency.

Apricots

Apricots look pretty on a shelf and equally pretty in a compote served in midwinter. We recommend canning those to be used for eating in salads or desserts and freezing those to be used in sauces, soufflés and pies. About 3 pounds of apricots should provide 4 pints of canned or frozen apricots.

CANNING

Prepare a mixture of 1 quart of cool water and 4 teaspoons of powdered ascorbic acid in a large bowl, to prevent darkening.

Wash the apricots, removing any stems. Do not peel.

Halve the apricots and remove the seeds. Drop the prepared fruit in the anti-darkening solution.

Prepare the canning liquid of your choice and bring it to the boiling point. It can be:

(1) 3 cups orange juice, or

(2) ½ cup sugar, ½ cup honey and 2 cups water, or

(3) 1 cup sugar and 2½ cups water.

Drain the apricots and place them in glass jars. If you want to take the time, line the outside of the jars decoratively by alternating the cut side of the fruit with the uncut side.

Pack the raw fruit within ¾ inch of the top of the jar. Pour in the boiling canning liquid to cover by ¼ inch, leaving ½ inch head space. Put on the lids and closures.

Place on a rack or in a steaming basket in a kettle of hot water. There should be an inch of water over the top of the jars. Bring to a boil and process for 25 minutes.

Remove the jars to a towel or rack and let stand until cold with air space in between the jars. Label and store.

FREEZING

Puree: About 1½ pounds of ripe apricots will make 2 pints of frozen puree. For convenience pack in 1 pint container and 2 ½-pint containers.

Prepare a mixture of ¼ teaspoon powdered ascorbic acid (vitamin C) with 4 tablespoons of water, to prevent darkening.

Wash the apricots well. Cut into quarters, removing the pit, but do not peel.

To puree the apricots, put them through a food mill or processor, or use the back of a spoon to force them through a strainer into a bowl. Quickly add the ascorbic acid mixture and 1 cup of sugar. Mix well.

Pack into 1 pint container and 2 ½-pint containers, leaving ½ inch head space. Label and freeze.

Apricot Compote

This refreshing dessert is prepared in two parts. The apricots and grapefruit are prepared with the sauce and refrigerated in advance. The raspberries are thawed and added just before serving time.

1 pint canned apricots	3 tablespoons light honey
1 pint canned grapefruit sections (in light syrup)	½ cup sweet white wine or sherry
2 tablespoons lemon juice	½ cup shredded coconut (optional)

Drain the canned apricot juice into a saucepan, and put the apricots in a pretty dessert bowl. Drain the grapefruit juice into the same saucepan, and add the sections to the apricots in the bowl.

Add the lemon juice and honey to the juices and boil down to half the original quantity. Cool and add the white wine. Pour over the fruit and refrigerate.

About 45 minutes before serving time, spread the raspberries on a baking sheet and thaw at room temperature. Gently fold the raspberries into the other fruits. Cover with shredded coconut if desired.

Serves 6 persons.

Frozen Apricot Bombe

The only trick to this splendid but very simple dessert is to remember to take the apricot puree out of the freezer in time to thaw. Other than that, this dessert can be prepared in 5 minutes.

1 pint apricot puree	2 tablespoons Cointreau or Triple Sec
½ pint apricot puree	
1 pint whipping cream	½ teaspoon almond extract
½ cup confectioner's sugar, sifted	½ cup slivered almonds

Thaw the puree.

Whip the cream until stiff. Fold in the sifted sugar and the almond extract. Fold in the pint of apricot puree.

Rinse a melon mold or other decorative mold briefly in cold water. Fill the mold with the mixture and cover with two thicknesses of aluminum foil. Freeze for 4 to 6 hours (or longer).

Mix the ½ pint of apricot puree with the orange liqueur. Cover and keep in the refrigerator.

To Serve: Dip the mold in lukewarm water for 30 seconds. Unmold onto a dessert platter. Cover with the apricot sauce and sprinkle with slivered almonds. The perfect accompaniment to this dessert is a macaroon.

Serves 8 to 10 persons.

Blackberries

When the raspberries, strawberries and blueberries have all gone by, there are still the humble blackberries to pick if you are brave and well protected against their thorny defense. We recommend having a couple of pints on hand if only to make an old-fashioned Blackberry Cobbler. It is equally good with canned or frozen blackberries, and if the seeds present a problem you can freeze the berries in puree form.

CANNING

Pick or buy 3 pints of blackberries. Pick them over to remove any immature or overripe berries. Wash well and drain.

Put the berries into 2 clean 1-pint jars, tapping the jars gently on the working surface to settle the berries.

Crush any remaining berries through a food mill or strainer to extract the juice. Add enough water to measure 1½ cups.

Add ¾ cup of sugar or ½ cup of light honey. Bring to a boil, and fill the jars with the boiling syrup up to within ½ inch of the top. Put on the lids and closures.

Place the jars in a steaming basket or on a rack in a kettle of very hot water. The water should cover the jar tops by at least 1 inch. Bring to a boil and process 10 minutes. Remove to a towel or rack, leaving space between the jars, and cool completely before labeling and storing.

FREEZING

Sweetened: Prepare the berries and the syrup in the same manner as for canning, except that the syrup must be allowed to cool completely before being poured over the berries. Pack the berries in the juice in plastic or glass containers, leaving a head space of ½ inch. Seal, label and freeze.

Sweetened pureed: Prepare the berries as for canning. Force them through a food mill or strainer. You should have almost 2 pints of puree. Add 1 cup of sugar and stir until the sugar disappears. Pack into plastic or glass containers, leaving ½ inch of head space. Seal, label and freeze.

Unsweetened: Pick over 1 quart of berries, removing any immature or overripe berries. Wash and drain very well, shaking the strainer to remove all possible moisture. Pack into plastic or glass containers, leaving ½ inch of head space. Seal and freeze.

Old-Fashioned Blackberry Cobbler

1   pint sweetened canned or
    frozen (thawed) blackberries
1   egg, well beaten
2   tablespoons butter or
    margarine
1   package (8-ounce) chilled
    baking powder biscuits
1   tablespoon melted butter

SAUCE:
½   cup honey
2   teaspoons lemon juice
2   teaspoons cornstarch
2   tablespoons melted butter
½   cup boiling water

Preheat the oven to 450 degrees F.

Mix the blackberries with the beaten egg and spread in the bottom of a buttered baking-serving dish. Dot with butter or margarine.

Divide the package of dough into half the normal biscuit pieces and spread over the top of the blackberries. Brush with melted butter. Bake 10 to 12 minutes. Serve warm (not hot) with the sauce.

Sauce: Stir the honey and lemon juice until well blended. Stir the cornstarch and butter together and add to the honey. Add the boiling water and bring to a boil. Simmer very gently for 3 to 4 minutes until clear.

Serves 4 persons.

Blueberries

In certain parts of the country, blueberry picking is a favorite summer pastime and preserving some of them for winter use is irresistible. There is no easier fruit to preserve. Our suggestion is to can or freeze them without sugar. They can then be eaten like fresh blueberries, sweetened or unsweetened, or they can be cooked in muffins, cobblers or cottage puddings. For pies we prefer to make the blueberry pie filling. Freeze it in an aluminum-foil pie tin, and then slip it into an unbaked pie shell at baking time.

During the blueberry season, process 1 quart of berries a day, canning the berries one day and freezing them the next. Each quart of berries will yield 1 pint for desserts, plus ½ pint for muffins. Count on a full quart for pie filling.

CANNING

Prepare your glass jars—a pint jar and a ½-pint jar.

Bring a full kettle of water to a boil.

Pick over the berries, removing any leaves or imperfect berries or twigs. Store-bought berries are usually winnowed before sale and do not need much attention. Wash them quickly in cool water and place in a fine mesh steaming basket or in a cheesecloth bag. Hold the basket or bag of berries in boiling water for just 1 minute. Remove and plunge into very cold water. Place the basket or bag over a bowl.

Carefully spoon the berries into the jars, taking care not to crush them. Leave ½ inch head room. Put on the lids and closures.

Place the jars in the steaming basket and lower basket into the same kettle of hot water. Bring to a boil and process 15 minutes. Remove from the water and cool completely before labeling and storing.

FREEZING

Prepare the berries as if for canning but do not blanch them. Pack them raw into pint and ½-pint containers, leaving ½ inch of head space. Seal, label and freeze.

Blueberry Muffins

If you are going to make blueberry muffins for breakfast, the night before combine the dry ingredients in one bowl and the wet ingredients (except for the butter) in another. That way, your ingredients will be at the proper room temperature and your work will be at a minimum at that moment of the day when food preparations seem the hardest for most people. If using frozen berries, take them out in the morning. Break them up in a small dish.

1¾ cups unbleached flour or	¾ cup milk
2 cups whole wheat	2 eggs
pastry flour	2 tablespoons melted butter
2 tablespoons sugar	or margarine
2 teaspoons baking powder	½ pint canned or frozen
½ teaspoon salt	(unthawed) blueberries

Preheat the oven to 400 degrees F.

Grease muffin tins unless they are of the special nonstick variety.

Combine the flour, sugar, baking powder and salt in a mixing bowl.

Beat the eggs and milk with a rotary beater until well blended. Add the melted butter or margarine.

Dredge the blueberries with a little flour. Combine the mixtures and add the berries, stirring as briefly as possible. The dough will seem lumpy—which it should.

Fill the muffin tins two-thirds full. Bake 20 minutes. Serve with butter, margarine or with cottage cheese.

Makes 16 3-inch muffins.

Frozen Blueberry Pie Filling

1 quart fresh blueberries	½ teaspoon cinnamon
¾ cup sugar	¼ teaspoon salt
1 tablespoon grated orange rind	4 tablespoons orange juice
	2 tablespoons cornstarch
⅛ teaspoon nutmeg	

Pick over the berries to remove all leaves, twigs or imperfect berries.

In an enamel-lined saucepan combine the sugar, orange rind, spices, salt and the orange juice previously mixed with the cornstarch.

Mix well and add the berries. Cook over moderate heat, stirring until the mixture comes to a full boil. Remove from the heat and pour into a 9-inch aluminum-foil pie plate. (We recommend nesting two plates together for firmer handling.) Cool and then chill. Wrap in a double thickness of aluminum foil. Label and freeze.

Blueberry Pie

Line a 9-inch pie tin with homemade or store-bought pastry. Slip the frozen pie filling into the pie shell. Pour over it 2 tablespoons of melted butter or margarine. Moisten the pastry rim and cover with a pastry circle. Press the edges together with the tines of a fork, and pierce the top in several places. Bake at 450 degrees F. for 10 minutes. Reduce the heat and bake 40 minutes at 350 degrees F.

Cherries

Pitting cherries is a bit of a chore and a bit of a bore, but a jar or two of canned dark red cherries, ready for Cherries Jubilee, can make any meal a glamorous feast. Canning is much better than freezing.

Choose a good TV program or turn on your favorite record when you pit the cherries. Unless you have inherited a cherry pitter, dip a couple of paper clips in boiling water to sterilize them and pit the cherries by inserting the rounded end into the stem end of the cherries. You will have your cherries pitted before you know it. Allow 2½ to 3 pounds of cherries for 2 pints of pitted cherries. If you prefer small parties, you may want to use ½-pint jars.

CANNING

Cold Pack: Wash the cherries and remove the stems. Drain well and pit them.

Make a sugar syrup using 1¼ cups of water and ½ cup of sugar. Bring to a boil and pour ½ cup in each pint jar (¼ cup for ½-pint jars). Drop cherries into the jars, tapping them lightly to settle the fruit. Do not press down. Fill the jars to within ¾ inch of the top. Add the remaining syrup and, if necessary, boiling water to cover the cherries, leaving ½ inch of head space. Insert a plastic or wooden knife to release air bubbles. Adjust the lids and screw bands.

Place on a rack or in a steaming basket in a kettle of hot water deep enough to cover the jars by 1 inch. Process for 20 minutes.

Hot Pack: Wash, stem, drain and pit the cherries as above. Place in an enamel-lined saucepan and mix gently with 4 tablespoons of water and 8 tablespoons of sugar. Stir carefully over moderate heat until the mixture is hot. Fill hot, clean jars with the mixture, leaving ½ inch head space. If there is not enough syrup to cover the cherries, add boiling water to within ½ inch of the top of the jars. Adjust lids and screw bands. Process 10 minutes in a boiling water bath.

Sugarless Pack: Prepare the cherries as for Cold Pack.

Instead of syrup use heated unsweetened orange juice so that the juice covers the cherries by ½ inch, leaving ½ inch head space. Process 20 minutes in the boiling water bath.

Cherries Jubilee

Cherries Jubilee can be served as is or with vanilla ice cream or over pound cake or with both. It is spectacular as well as delectable.

1 pint canned cherries	2 tablespoons kirsch
½ teaspoon cornstarch	or other cherry brandy
1 tablespoon water	1½ quarts vanilla
4 tablespoons Cointreau	ice cream (optional)
or other orange liqueur	8 slices Pound
	Cake (optional)

Pour the liquid from the canned cherries into a serving saucepan or, better still, in the top of a chafing dish. Bring to a boil. Add the cornstarch mixed with the water and cook until clear. Remove from the heat and stir in the cherries. Let stand at room temperature.

Pour the liqueurs into a small heatproof pitcher or tiny saucepan.

To serve: Heat the cherries in the chafing dish or serving saucepan, preferably at the table. At the same time warm the liqueurs. Pour the liqueurs over the hot cherries and immediately light with a match. Spoon the liqueurs over the cherries for a moment, and serve still flaming in individual dishes or over ice cream and/or cake.

Serves 8 persons.

Cranberries

There are some people we know who will not eat turkey unless cranberry sauce is on the table. There are others who drink cranberry juice for the vitamin C content and other beneficial qualities. Our favorite cranberry preparation is a sherbet served halfway through a large Thanksgiving or Christmas dinner. Known in rarefied gastronomical circles as a "remove," it is designed to freshen the palate for food still to come.

Canned Jellied Cranberry Sauce

1 pint cranberries	1 cup sugar
¾ cup water	2 slices of orange

Wash the berries, removing any stems or imperfect berries.

Place in a small saucepan with cold water, the sugar and orange slices (with peel). Bring to a boil over moderate heat, stirring until the sugar is dissolved. Cook until the skins burst.

Remove the orange slices and force the cranberries through a food mill or strainer.

Reheat the juice and cook until the jelly sheets from a metal spoon or until it registers 220 degrees F. on a candy thermometer.

Pour into 3 hot, clean ½-pint jelly jars, leaving ¼ inch head space. Put on the lids and closures. Place on a rack or in a steaming basket in a kettle of almost-boiling water. The water should cover the tops of the jars by 1 inch. Bring to a boil and process 10 minutes.

Remove the jars to a rack or towel, leaving space between jars to cool. Label and store.

Canned Whole Cranberry Sauce

This is so quickly made that it is a good idea to begin heating the processing water when you start the recipe.

2 *cups cranberries*	⅛ *stick cinnamon*
1 *cup sugar*	2 *cloves*
1 *cup water*	

Wash the cranberries, removing any imperfect berries and other foreign material.

Place the sugar, water and spices (enclosed in a stainless steel tea ball) in a saucepan. Bring to a boil, stirring until the sugar dissolves, and cook 3 minutes. Add the cranberries. Cook until the berries burst.

Remove the tea ball and pour the sauce into 3 hot, clean ½-pint jelly jars. Put on the lids and closures.

Place the jars on a rack or in a steaming basket and process in the boiling water bath for 10 minutes. Remove the jars and cool completely before labeling and storing.

Canned Cranberry Juice

1 *quart cranberries*	*Sugar or artificial sweetener*
4 *cups water*	

Pick over the berries and wash them well. Place in a kettle with the water. Bring to a boil and cook until the berries are very soft.

Force through a food mill or coarse strainer.

Strain the resulting juice through a jelly bag or a colander lined with 4 thicknesses of cheesecloth.

Sweeten to taste with sugar or artificial sweetener.

Reheat without boiling and pour into 3 hot, clean pint jars or 4 12-ounce jars, leaving ¼ inch head room. Adjust the lids and closures.

Place the jars on a rack or in a steaming basket. Lower into almost boiling water to cover by 1 inch. Process 10 minutes.

Remove to a towel or rack, leaving space between the jars. Cool completely before labeling and storing.

Cranberry Sherbet

½ cup water
½ cup sugar
2 teaspoons unflavored gelatin
½ pint cranberry juice

½ cup orange juice
2 teaspoons grated orange rind
2 tablespoons dry vermouth

Bring the sugar and water to a boil and boil for 1 minute.

Meanwhile, soften the gelatin in 4 tablespoons of water and add to the boiled syrup. Stir until the gelatin is dissolved. Remove from the heat and stir in the cranberry juice, orange juice and rind and the vermouth. Taste for sweetness. The mixture should be on the tart side.

Pour the mixture into a freezing tray and set in the freezer for 20 to 25 minutes or until the edges are frozen to a mushy stage.

Place in the previously chilled bowl of an electric beater and beat hard (with previously chilled beaters) until smooth. This should take a matter of seconds. Return to tray, cover and put back in the freezer. Stir twice during the freezing process. Use the sherbet within 24 hours if possible.

Serves 4 to 6 persons.

Guavas

Guavas are a tropical fruit that have found their way to the markets of the north. Everyone thinks of guava jelly but canned guavas make a lovely ready-to-eat dessert, which will cause a lot of appreciative comment. Two and one-half pounds of guavas should yield 2 pints of processed guava. We recommend raw packing for this fruit.

CANNING

Wash the guavas well. Cut off the ends and peel as close to the flesh as possible. Slice like peaches, or halve and remove the seeds. Drop the guavas into pint jars.

Fill the jars within ½ inch of the top with one of the following canning liquids: (a) 1¼ cups water plus ½ cup sugar brought to the boiling point, or (b) 12 ounces unsweetened pineapple juice brought to the boiling point.

Insert a wooden or plastic knife to remove air bubbles.

Put the lids and screw bands in place, and lower the jars into a kettle of hot water deep enough to cover them by 1 inch. Bring the water to a boil and process for 15 minutes.

Remove the jars to a rack or towel, leaving air space between the jars, and allow to cool. Label and store.

Hot Guava Compote

1 pint canned guavas	4 tablespoons butter or
1 teaspoon cornstarch	margarine, melted
1 tablespoon water	½ teaspoon cinnamon
1 teaspoon lemon juice	¼ teaspoon powdered cloves
1 cup vanilla wafer crumbs	Dairy sour cream or heavy
	cream (optional)

Drain the liquid from the jar into a saucepan. Bring to a boil. Add the cornstarch mixed with the water and cook until clear. Remove from the heat and add the lemon juice.

Place the guavas in a shallow baking-serving dish. Cover with the syrup and let cool.

Pulverize the cookies into crumbs with a blender or food processor.

Toss with the butter or margarine and the spices. Spread over the guavas.

Twenty minutes before serving, bake the guavas at 350 degrees F. Serve plain or with the cream of your choice.

Serves 4 persons.

Nectarines

Follow directions for canning and freezing peaches. Recipes for peaches and nectarines can be used interchangeably. A pint of nectarines combined with a pint of canned or frozen blueberries makes a delicious compote, and when served with a generous blessing of apricot brandy it becomes party fare.

Nectarine Charlotte

1 pint sliced nectarines, canned or frozen (thawed)	½ pint whipping cream
1 8-ounce package ladyfingers	4 tablespoons sifted confectioners' sugar
½ cup peach brandy	¼ teaspoon vanilla

Drain the nectarines and boil down the syrup to ⅓ its original quantity.

Reserve 4 slices of nectarine. Cut the rest rather coarsely.

Split the ladyfingers and dip each half briefly in the brandy.

Line the bottom and sides of a small charlotte mold or soufflé dish with the ladyfinger halves, rounded side out.

Whip ¾ cup of the cream and sweeten with 3 tablespoons of sugar and 2 teaspoons of the brandy. Add the cut fruit and mix briefly.

Put half of the filling in the mold and top with moistened ladyfingers. Fill with the rest of the cream mixture and top with ladyfingers. Cover with a round of wax paper and aluminum foil. Place in the refrigerator for several hours.

Put the remaining brandy and reduced syrup in a small bowl and soak the 4 nectarine slices.

To serve: Whip the remaining cream until stiff. Sweeten with 1 tablespoon of sugar and the vanilla. Unmold the dessert on a round platter. Pipe the whipped cream around the top and bottom. Garnish with the nectarines and dribble the syrup over the top.

Serves 4 persons.

Peaches

Canned and frozen peaches are what most beginning canners start with. They are very reassuring because it's hard to fail with them, and because there are so many ways to serve them—straight from the canning jar or thawed from the freezing container, combined with other fruits to make a fruit compote or salad, or dressed up in a sherry custard. If possible, use local tree-ripened peaches. Three pounds or approximately 1 dozen peaches should yield 3 pints of canned or frozen fruit. We recommend cold-packing 3 pints of halved or sliced peaches one day and, on another day, freezing an equal amount of slices or pureed fruit. Pureed peaches are excellent for soufflés and mousses. Follow these simple directions to use a minimum of space and equipment.

CANNING

Bring a kettle three-quarters full of water to a boil. This water will be used for loosening the skins of the peaches and for canning.

Wash 3 pint jars with lids and screw bands in hot sudsy water and drain them, or better yet run them through the dishwasher when you are washing the breakfast or dinner dishes. Leave the jars and closures in the dishwasher, or in hot water, until they are needed.

Put a quart of water in a bowl. Add 4 teaspoons of crystalline ascorbic acid or ½ tablespoon of salt and ½ tablespoon of vinegar or lemon juice and mix well. This solution will help to keep the peaches from darkening as you prepare them.

Wash and drain the peaches. Fill the kitchen sink with cold water.

Put half the peaches in a canning/steaming basket. Lower them into the boiling water for 30 seconds. Quickly plunge them into the cold water. Repeat the process with the rest of the peaches. Turn off the heat under the kettle.

Slip the skin from a peach. Halve it, remove the pit and scoop out the rosy fibrous center. It's delicious to taste but tends to darken the color of the canned peach. Leave the peaches in halves or slice them as you prefer. Place them in solution. Repeat the process until all the peaches are prepared.

Prepare and bring to a boil one of the following canning liquids: (a) ½ cup sugar and 1¼ cups water, or (b) ¼ cup sugar, ¼ cup honey and 1 cup water, or (c) 12 ounces unsweetened pineapple juice.

Drain the peaches and fill the jars. If packing halves, place the peaches cavity side down. Fill to within ¾ inch from the top. Pour in the preferred canning liquid to cover, leaving ½ inch head space.

Insert a wooden or plastic knife into the jars to release air bubbles. Add more canning liquid if needed.

Wipe the tops of the jars with a damp paper towel. Put on the lids and screw on the bands firmly.

Place the jars in a steaming basket or on a rack in the kettle of hot water. The water should cover the jars by at least 1 inch. Add more hot water if necessary. Cover and bring the water to a boil. Process 25 minutes.

Remove the jars from the kettle and place on a damp towel or on a rack to cool, with air space between the jars. When they are completely cooled, remove the screw bands, label and store in a dark cupboard.

FREEZING.

Sliced Peaches: Prepare 6 cups of sliced peaches as if for canning, but do not use the anti-darkening solution. Slice the peaches directly into a bowl with 1 cup of sugar mixed with ⅜ teaspoon of crystalline ascorbic acid. Stir gently until mixed. Let stand until some syrup is formed (5 to 10 minutes). Spoon the peaches and the syrup into scrupulously clean freezer jars or containers, leaving ¼ inch head space. Seal, label and freeze.

Pureed Peaches: Wash, skin and pit 1 pound of peaches (4 medium-size peaches). Remove the fibrous center with a metal spoon and slice into the blender or food processor. Add ¼ teaspoon of crystalline ascorbic acid and 1 tablespoon of sugar, if desired.

Puree and quickly transfer to a 12-ounce jar or container. Cover with plastic wrap and then with the container top. This will help prevent darkening. Label and freeze.

Canned Peaches with Sherry Custard Sauce

4 egg yolks	Slivered almonds
½ cup sugar	1 pint canned or frozen
½ cup sherry	peaches (thawed)
1½ teaspoons lemon juice	

Using a rotary egg beater, beat the egg yolks and sugar in the top part of a double boiler over 2 inches of simmering water. When the sauce begins to thicken, add the sherry while still beating. When the sauce has the thickness of heavy cream, remove from the heat and add the lemon juice.

Serve the custard warm over chilled peaches and sprinkle with slivered almonds.

Serves 4 persons.

Pears

Pears seem more satisfactory canned than frozen. The only difficult part is to get pears at their peak of perfection. They ripen very quickly, so it is best to pick them or buy them when they are slightly underripe and to watch them like a hawk so that they will be in the can before they are too ripe. Pears make a fine dessert when served with a claret sauce, spiced with cinnamon, or topped with a ginger sauce. Canned pears served in salad bring a refreshing note to lunch or dinner. Allow 3 to 4 pounds of medium-size pears to make 3 pints when canned.

CANNING

Mix 1 quart of water and 4 teaspoons of crystalline ascorbic acid in a bowl.

Wash the pears well. Peel them and cut them in half. Scoop out the center core with a small spoon. Place the pears as they are prepared in the anti-darkening solution. Do not let them stand more than 20 minutes.

Cold Pack: Prepare a canning liquid by bringing to a boil one of the following: (a) ½ cup sugar and 1¼ cups of water, or (b) ¼ cup sugar, ¼ cup light honey and 1 cup of water, or (c) 12 ounces unsweetened grapefruit or pineapple juice.

Fill the hot, clean jars with the pear halves, leaving ¾ inch head space. Fill with the preferred canning liquid within ½ inch of the top. Insert a wooden or plastic knife to remove air bubbles. Put on the lids and screw on the bands tightly.

Place the jars on a rack or in a steaming basket in a kettle of hot water deep enough to cover the jars by 1 inch. Process 25 minutes. Remove the jars to a rack or damp towel and cool completely with air space between the jars. Label and store in a dark cupboard.

Hot Pack: Prepare one of the canning liquids and bring to a boil.

Add the drained pear halves and bring back to a boil. Simmer very gently for 5 minutes.

Spoon the pears and the syrup into the jars, leaving ½ inch head space. Insert a wooden or plastic knife around the jars to release air bubbles. Add more canning liquid if necessary. Put on the lids and screw bands.

Place the jars on a rack or in a steaming basket with 1 inch of water to cover in the boiling water bath and process for 20 minutes.

Remove the jars and cool as for Cold Pack.

Watercress and Pear Salad, Gorgonzola

1 *bunch watercress*	2 *tablespoons wine vinegar*
4 *ounces cream cheese*	6 *tablespoons salad oil*
4 *ounces Gorgonzola cheese*	2 *teaspoons chopped pimiento*
8 *canned pear halves*	*Salt and black pepper*

Soak the watercress in cold water for 15 minutes. Lift out of the water and remove any bruised leaves or very coarse stems. Shake very dry and chill in the refrigerator.

Cream together the cream cheese and half the Gorgonzola. (Roquefort can be substituted for the Gorgonzola.)

Drain the pears and fill the cavities with the cheese mixture. Chill in the refrigerator.

In a small bowl, mix the vinegar, oil and pimientos. Crumble the remaining Gorgonzola into the dressing before seasoning to taste with salt and freshly ground black pepper.

To serve: Line 4 salad plates with the watercress. Put 2 pear halves cut side down on each plate. Stir the dressing and spoon it over the pears.

Serves 4 persons.

Plums

A few jars of greengage or meaty dark purple plums, whether canned or frozen, can add variety to winter meals. We recommend canning them raw pack or freezing them in halves or quarters for pies or compotes, or in puree for serving over ice cream or custard-filled cream puffs. Pick fully ripe but not soft fruit. Allow 1½ to 2½ pounds of plums for 2 pints canned, 2 to 3 pounds for 2 pints frozen.

CANNING

Prepare the canning liquid by bringing to a boil one of the following: (a) ½ cup sugar and 1¼ cups water or (b) ¼ cup sugar, ¼ cup honey and 1 cup water, or (c) 12 ounces unsweetened pineapple juice.

Wash the fruit well and drain it. If leaving the fruit whole, prick the skin with a needle to keep the plums from bursting. If using the freestone variety, you may cut them in halves or quarters and remove the pit. Place the fruit in hot, clean canning jars, filling within ¾ inch of the top. Cover with the canning liquid. Put on the tops and screw bands. Lower the jars in a steaming basket or place on a rack in a kettle of hot water deep enough to cover the cans by at least 1 inch. Bring to a boil and process for 20 minutes.

Remove the jars to a damp towel or rack with air space between the jars to cool completely. Label and store.

FREEZING

Sweetened: Prepare canning liquid (a) or (b). Let cool completely.

Wash the plums well and pat dry with toweling. Do not prick the skins. If desired, cut into halves or sections and remove the pit. Put the fruit in plastic or glass freezing containers.

Stir ¼ teaspoon of crystalline ascorbic acid into the cooled syrup until dissolved. Pour the syrup over the plums, leaving ½ inch head space. Seal, label and place in freezer.

FREEZING

Unsweetened: Wash the plums and dry them well. Do not prick them or cut them. Pack into plastic freezer bags. Expel most of the air from the bags. Tie the tops very tightly and freeze.

Pureed (2 pints): Wash 2 pounds of plums. Dry them and cut into halves to remove the pits. Force the fruit through a food mill.

Stir in 8 to 10 tablespoons of sugar and ¼ teaspoon crystalline ascorbic acid until dissolved. Fill the containers, leaving ½ inch head space. Seal, label and freeze.

Plum Almond Compote

Drain the syrup from 1 pint canned or frozen plums and boil the syrup down to half its original volume. Remove from the heat and stir in 2 tablespoons of kirsch or cherry brandy.

Remove the pits if necessary and fill the pit spaces with whole skinless almonds.

Place the plums in dessert dishes and pour the syrup over them.

Sprinkle lightly with slivered almonds. Serve very cold.

Serves 4 persons.

Raspberries

Raspberries are so satisfactory when preserved by freezing that we do not recommend any other processing except making jams and jellies. If raspberries, wild or cultivated, are carefully picked, they can be dropped from bush to container, sealed, labeled and frozen. The secret of success is not in the freezing but in the thawing. If raspberries are to be eaten raw, the thawing must be carefully timed. About 40 minutes before they are to be eaten, spread them out on a baking sheet and let stand at room temperature. At dessert time they should still be whole, cool but not frozen. The time may vary slightly according to the temperature of the room. Served with a sprinkle of sugar and sweet or sour cream, raspberries will bring back summer memories more vividly than any other fruit. Pureed frozen raspberries make an excellent basis for sherbets, mousses, soufflés and sauces.

FREEZING

Frozen whole: Unless you are picking from bush to container, spread berries, a pint at a time, on a tray or baking sheet. Quickly pick out the fresh whole berries, leaving any leaves or broken berries in the tray.

Fill ½-pint and pint containers with the berries, leaving ½ inch head space. Seal, label and freeze.

Pick out the broken berries for pureeing.

Frozen pureed: Method 1: Pick over the fruit and force both whole and broken berries through a stainless steel food mill or strainer. Add 2 to 4 tablespoons of sugar to each cup of berries according to taste. Stir until the sugar dissolves, and pour into ½-pint and pint freezing jars or plastic containers, leaving ½ inch head space. Seal, label and freeze.

Method 2: Using a blender or a food processor, spin a pint of raspberries at a time with ⅓ to ½ cup of sugar and ½ teaspoon lemon juice to a puree. Strain the puree through a stainless steel sieve to remove the seeds. Pack as above and seal, label and freeze.

Raspberry Pear Delight

4 canned pear halves	1 pint lemon sherbet
½ pint raspberry puree	

Drain the syrup from the pears into a saucepan and boil down to 4 tablespoonfuls. Place the pear halves in a shallow dish and pour the reduced syrup over them. Chill in the refrigerator.

Thaw the puree.

To serve: Spoon ½ cup of lemon sherbet in each of 4 dessert dishes. Top with the pears and cover with the raspberry puree. Serve immediately.

Serves 4 persons.

Danish Raspberry Cream

1 pint frozen raspberries	4 tablespoons potato flour
2¼ cups water	4 tablespoons heavy cream
½ cup sugar	Slivered almonds
1 teaspoon lemon juice	(optional)

Bring the raspberries, 2 cups of the water, the lemon juice and sugar to a slow boil. Simmer 3 minutes.

Strain the raspberry mixture into another saucepan to remove the seeds.

Mix the potato flour with the remaining water and add to the raspberry mixture. Stir over moderate heat until the mixture thickens. Cool slightly.

Pour the mixture into individual dessert dishes. Cool and chill for several hours.

To serve: Pour a tablespoon of heavy cream over the surface of each serving. Sprinkle with slivered almonds if desired.

Variation: Substitute 1 jar (8 ounces) of currant jelly for 1 cup of water and the sugar.

Serves 4 persons.

Rhubarb

Rhubarb may well be the beginning of the canning season. It is best picked in early spring when the stalks are young and tender. In the old days it was considered a healthy restorative after the long winter months. Rhubarb sauce is a New England favorite, and a pie filled with a combination of strawberries and rhubarb makes a superb ending to any meal. We recommend canning rhubarb sauce and freezing rhubarb unsweetened for use in pies and cakes. About 2 pounds of rhubarb will yield 1 quart of prepared rhubarb.

CANNING

Choose tender stalks. If only large stalks are available remove the tough fibers. Trim both ends of the stalks and wash well. Remember that rhubarb leaves can be poisonous and should be discarded immediately. Cut the rhubarb into 1-inch pieces.

Sweetened: Place the cut rhubarb in a glass or porcelain bowl. Add 2 to 4 tablespoons of sugar for each cup of rhubarb. Stir once and cover. Let stand 3 to 4 hours.

Bring the rhubarb to a full boil. Remove from the heat and pack into hot, clean ½-pint and pint jars, leaving ½ inch head space.

Put on the lids and screw bands tightly. Place on a rack or in a steaming basket in hot water deep enough to cover the jars by 1 inch. Bring to a boil and process for 10 minutes. Remove the jars to a damp towel or rack and cool completely before labeling and storing in a dark place.

FREEZING

Unsweetened: Prepare the rhubarb as for canning but do not add sugar. Place in 12-ounce (¾-pint) and pint containers, leaving ½ inch of head space. Tap the containers to settle the rhubarb in order to fill the containers well. Seal, label and freeze.

Rhubarb and Strawberry Pie

	Pie pastry (homemade or store-bought)	2	tablespoons cornstarch
		4	tablespoons water
1	pint frozen sugar-pack sliced strawberries	2	teaspoons grated orange rind
1	pint unsweetened frozen rhubarb	1	tablespoon butter or margarine
1	cup brown sugar		

Line a 9-inch pie plate with pastry, trimming the edges even with the rim. Brush the pastry with a little egg white. Place in the refrigerator.

Thaw the strawberries and rhubarb just enough to be able to mix them.

Combine the cornstarch and water in a 2-cup measure. When they are blended, stir in the brown sugar and orange rind. Combine the mixture with the fruit and let stand 10 minutes.

Preheat the oven to 425 degrees F.

Fill the pie shell and dot with butter.

Moisten the edge of the lower crust and cover with the top crust, pressing the edges together with the tines of a fork. Prick the top crust in several places.

Place the pie on a baking sheet to avoid any possible spillage. Bake 10 minutes. Reduce the heat to 375 degrees F. and bake 30 minutes longer.

Serves 6 to 8 persons.

Spring Rhubarb and Strawberry Sauce

Spring sauce is a New England tradition which is served when the strawberries first ripen in late spring. Thanks to canning and freezing it can now be enjoyed all winter long. It makes a refreshing ending to a large meal. Some people make a luncheon of homemade bread and butter and plenty of Spring sauce.

1 *pint canned rhubarb*   1 *pint frozen strawberries*

Combine the canned fruit with the strawberries which are *just* thawed. Serve well chilled in individual dessert glasses.

Serves 4 persons.

Rhubarb Cake

24	ounces (3 cups) *unsweetened frozen rhubarb*	
2	cups unbleached flour	
1½	teaspoons baking soda	
½	teaspoon salt	
1	stick (8 ounces) butter or margarine	
1½	cups brown sugar	
1	large egg	
1	cup milk	

TOPPING:

½ cup brown sugar
2 teaspoons unbleached or whole wheat pastry flour
1 teaspoon vanilla
1 teaspoon cinnamon
½ cup chopped nuts

Preheat the oven to 350 degrees F. Grease a 9-by-12-inch oven-serving dish. Thaw and drain the rhubarb. Pat dry with toweling. Combine and sift the flour, soda and salt. Cream the butter or margarine and sugar in a bowl with an electric beater. Add the egg and beat until smooth. Add the milk and dry ingredients alternately, and when they are well blended, fold in the rhubarb.

Spread in the prepared dish.

In a small bowl toss the sugar, flour, vanilla, cinnamon and nuts until mixed. Sprinkle over the cake batter. Bake 35 minutes.

Serve cold without icing or warm with whipped cream.

Strawberries

Strawberries, like raspberries, are so much more satisfactory frozen than canned that we recommend freezing only. They may be packed unsweetened or sweetened, but the addition of a little sugar keeps their flavor garden fresh. Strawberries, if packed whole, should be covered with a syrup. The easiest method is to pack them sliced or halved with a little sugar. Pureed, they are the basis for all kinds of desserts, hot and cold. With sliced and whole berries, you are ready for wintertime strawberry shortcake, and you can flash-freeze separately a few perfect berries to use half-thawed as decorations for a festive dessert.

FREEZING

Unsweetened: Pack ripe but firm berries that have been washed, hulled and dried on toweling into plastic freezing bags. Expel as much air as possible from the bags. Seal, label and freeze.

Whole Sweetened Berries: Bring ¾ cup of sugar and 1 cup of water to a boil, stirring just until the sugar dissolves. Remove from the heat and cool completely.

Wash the berries briefly. Hull them and wash again. Drain well and place in ½-pint and pint containers, leaving ¾ inch head space. Fill with syrup up to within ½ inch of the top. Seal, label and freeze.

Sugar-Pack Sliced: Slice or halve the berries after washing and hulling from stem end down. Place the berries in a shallow bowl and sprinkle with sugar, allowing 3 tablespoons of sugar to a cup of fruit. Mix gently until the sugar disappears.

Pack into ½-pint and pint containers, leaving ½ inch head space. Seal, label and freeze.

Puree: Spin 1 pint of washed and hulled berries with 3 to 4 tablespoons of sugar, according to the sweetness of the berries, and 1 teaspoon of lemon juice. Pack the puree into ½-pint and pint containers, leaving ½ inch of head space. Seal, label and freeze.

Whole berries for decoration: Place large perfect berries that have been washed and hulled on a baking sheet or in a pie tin and place in the freezer. When they are solidly frozen, pack them in small plastic bags and expel most of the air from the bags. Use these berries in a semi-thawed condition to decorate cheesecake, soufflés or parfaits. If allowed to thaw completely, they will become soggy and shapeless.

Strawberry Mousse Ring

Sometimes the simplest recipes produce the best results. This one is a case in point. The mousse may be made days in advance if more convenient and if freezer space allows.

1 *pint frozen strawberry puree*	1 *teaspoon lemon juice*
½ *pint whipping cream*	4 *tablespoons light rum*
3 *very ripe bananas*	2 *tablespoons sugar (optional)*

Thaw the puree. Whip the cream and fold into the puree. Pour the mixture into a 6-cup ring mold. Cover with aluminum foil. Freeze for at least 4 hours.

Three hours before serving, peel and slice the bananas into a bowl. Stir in the lemon juice and rum. Cover and let stand at room temperature. Before serving, taste for sweetness.

To serve: Remove the foil from the mousse and dip the ring mold into lukewarm water very briefly. Turn the mousse out on a round dessert platter and fill the center with the bananas.

Serves 6 persons.

Jelly and Jam Specialties

Living in small quarters precludes the old-fashioned habit of making jams and jellies in large quantities, but even those with spacious kitchen and storage room are not making as much jelly as formerly—unless they are going through a peanut-butter-and-jelly-sandwich phase.

In part, this is due to growing awareness of the relationship between health problems and the consumption of large quantities of refined sugar; it is difficult to make good jelly without using a lot of sugar. Another reason is that when wine was frowned upon, jelly appeared on the dinner table as a kind of substitute; today more people are drinking wine with their meals and serving jelly only with the breakfast toast.

For those who must have grape and apple jelly on hand at all times of night and day, we suggest making both apple and grape juice along with the first small batch of apple and grape jelly. When that is depleted, it is easy to turn a pint of canned or frozen juice into jelly in the twinkling of an eye. This plan saves shelf space as well as glasses.

We give you recipes for some easy-to-make jellies and some very special jellies and jams, most of which will not be found on the grocery shelf. These are jellies for special occasions—some are made with sugar or honey and some with artificial sweetener.

Guidelines for Making Jellies and Preserves

QUANTITIES:

In the recipes that follow, 4 cups of prepared fruit or fruit juice is the largest quantity suggested for processing at one time.

CONTAINERS:

Plan to put up all of your jams and jellies in glass jars intended for home food preserving, with self-adhesive lids and reusable screw bands. This is much safer than the old-fashioned way of filling odd glasses and topping them with paraffin. Ordinary glasses and jars may crack when filled with hot jelly. Paraffin is possible but precarious—it catches fire so easily that melting it on the kitchen stove is dangerous, and it does not always make a seal that is tight enough to keep jelly from spoiling, especially if the jelly must be stored at room temperature. On the other hand, if you use nick-free canning jars and the proper lids, and follow directions, success is assured.

EQUIPMENT:

You will need a saucepan and a kettle, a small set of kitchen scales (there is a good one just 6 inches in diameter) and a ladle. A candy thermometer is not expensive and it will take all the guesswork out of making preserves. A timer is essential, but most stoves are equipped with timers that will serve the purpose.

PLANNING:

If jelly-making is to be easy and pleasant and not interfere with other kitchen activities, timing is important. One good plan is to prepare the fruit or fruit juice the first thing in the morning. Put the jars, lids and screw bands you will need through the dishwasher along with the breakfast dishes; if you leave the dishwasher closed, the jars will stay clean and hot until you are ready to fill them. Or, wash the jars and closures in soapy water and then keep them in a pan of hot water over low heat until you are ready for them.

SEALING:

For safe sealing, fill jars almost to the top with the hot jelly or preserves (see directions). If you haven't enough to fill the last jar to the proper level, store that jar in the refrigerator and plan to use the contents promptly, perhaps to make a dessert such as tarts or a jelly roll.

HOT-WATER-BATH CANNING:

Jelly does not need further processing, but it is recommended that jams, preserves and fruit butters go through the hot water bath canning process. For times, see directions.

Easy Fruit and Berry Jellies

Apple Jelly

It is good that apple jelly falls at the head of the alphabet because it is the perfect beginning to jelly-making. Apples have so much natural pectin that their jelly is failproof. The flavor of the jelly will vary somewhat according to the apples that are used. To make sure that there is enough pectin, include some underripe apples. Apple jelly can be the basis of other delicate jellies—such as mint, tarragon and rose geranium.

Arrange the equipment so that everything you need is at hand, and wash the jars and closures either by hand or in the dishwasher. They should be kept hot until filled.

4-5 pounds apples	¼ teaspoon crystalline
4-5 cups water	ascorbic acid
Sugar	

To extract the juice: Wash the apples well, removing any bruised spot as well as the stem and blossom ends. Cut the apples into wedges without peeling or coring and put with water in a kettle and bring to a boil. Cook gently for 20 minutes or until the apples are very soft.

Unless you have a jelly bag and jelly-bag standard, simply line a colander with 2 or 3 layers of cheesecloth and suspend the colander over a china or stainless steel bowl. Fill the colander with the cooked apples and let drip for 2 hours or until the apples are dry.

Preheat the oven to 350 degrees F.

Measure the juice. You should have 4 cups. If there is not quite enough juice, squeeze the apples to press out a little more. Before adding it to the clear juice, re-strain it through clean cheesecloth or a spotlessly clean old dish towel.

Measure sugar into a pie tin, allowing ¾ cup of sugar to every cup of juice. Place in the oven until warm.

Combine the juice and sugar in a stainless steel or aluminum sauce-pan with the ascorbic acid. Stir until the mixture boils. Cook over high heat until the syrup measures 220 degrees F. on a thermometer or until the jelly "sheets" from a metal spoon. This means that you dip a cold spoon into the jelly and hold it up 12 to 15 inches above the pan so that the side is parallel to the cooking syrup. If the drops flow together and fall off the spoon, the jelly is ready. A thermometer, however, is more reliable.

Remove the jelly from the heat and skim off any froth on the surface.

Pour the jelly into the jars, leaving ⅛ inch head room. Wipe the rims clean and put on the lids and screw bands. Cool 12 hours on a rack, leaving air space between the jars. Label and store in a cool dark place.

Makes 4 8-ounce jars.

Apple Mint Jelly

Prepare the apple jelly according to directions. Remove the froth from the surface and add ½ cup of freshly washed and slightly bruised mint leaves and 5 or 6 drops of green food coloring. Stir over moderate heat for 1 minute. Strain into prepared jars, filling them within ⅛ inch of the rim. Quickly wipe off the rim of each jar. Drop a fresh mint leaf in each and put on the lids and screw bands. Let stand for 12 hours. Label and store.

Apple Tarragon Jelly

Prepare the apple jelly according to directions. Remove the froth, and add ⅓ cup freshly washed tarragon leaves and 2 or 3 drops of green vegetable coloring. Stir over moderate heat for 1 minute. Strain into prepared jars, filling them to within ⅛ inch of the top. Add 2 or 3 tarragon leaves to each jar. Wipe the rims with a damp towel and put on the lids and the closures. Let stand without moving for 12 hours. Label and store.

Rose Geranium Jelly

Many people grow the rose geranium as an indoor plant. Its lovely pink blossom is what the jelly tries to approximate.

Prepare the apple jelly according to directions. Remove the froth, and add 2 rose geranium leaves that have been washed and dried. Add 3 or 4 drops of red coloring. Cook 1 minute over moderate heat. Strain the syrup into the prepared jars and add a small piece of geranium leaf to each. Wipe off rims of the jars and put on the lids and closures. Let stand for 12 hours without moving. Label and store.

Four-in-One Apple Jellies

It is amusing to make four kinds of jelly at one time and it is very easy, requiring very little extra time and only a saucepan for added equipment. We suggest 1 jar of rose geranium, 1 jar of apple tarragon, 1 jar of apple mint and 1 jar of apple jelly. The result is a jewel-like collection.

Have all your equipment organized and the required leaves, jars and jar closures washed and ready.

Prepare the apple jelly according to directions. Remove any froth on top of the hot apple syrup and keep it warm (but not boiling).

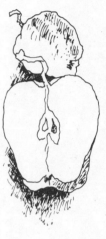

Rose Geranium: Pour 1 cup of apple syrup into a small deep saucepan. Bring to a boil. Add 1 or 2 drops of red coloring to the syrup (it should be pale pink). Using a silver fork or wooden spear, swish 2 rose geranium leaves in the boiling syrup just until you can smell it. Remove the leaves and pour the syrup into a prepared jar. Add a small piece of leaf and wipe off the rim of the jar. Put on the lid and closure.

Apple Tarragon: Pour another cup of syrup into the saucepan. Add 1 small drop of green vegetable coloring to the boiling syrup. Holding a large sprig of tarragon by the stem, swirl the tarragon leaves into the syrup for not more than 1 minute. Withdraw the tarragon and pour into a jar. Wipe off the rim with a damp cloth and add 1 or 2 leaves of tarragon. Put on the lid and closure.

Apple Mint: Pour a third cup of syrup into the saucepan. Bring to a boil. Add 2 or 3 drops of green vegetable coloring. Holding a bunch of mint leaves by the stems, swirl them around in the syrup until you smell the mint. Withdraw the leaves and fill a jelly jar with the syrup. Add 1 small mint leaf, wipe off the rim and cover with lid and closure.

Bring the remaining cup of syrup just to a boil. Pour it into the remaining jar. Wipe the rim and put on the lid.

Screw the bands firmly on all the jars and let stand 12 hours before labeling and storing in a dark, cool place.

Makes 4 8-ounce jars.

Christmas Jelly

This crimson-colored and well-spiced jelly makes a welcome Christmas gift and is a pleasant addition to all holiday menus.

Apple jelly	⅛ teaspoon allspice
2 teaspoons cinnamon	Red coloring
½ teaspoon cloves	

Make the apple jelly according to directions, adding the spices when adding the sugar. Use enough red vegetable coloring to make the jelly deep red.

Pour the jelly into prepared decorative jelly jars. Put on the lids and screw bands and let stand without moving for 12 hours. Label with a Christmas seal and store in a dark, cool place.

Makes 4 8-ounce jars.

Apple Juice for Future Jelly

6 pounds apples	6 cups water

Wash the apples, removing the stem and blossom ends. Cut the apples into pieces and drop them into a kettle. Add the water and bring to a boil. Cover and cook gently for 20 minutes or until the apples are very soft.

Line a colander with 4 thicknesses of dampened cheesecloth or with a dampened clean old dish towel. Suspend it over a bowl. Pour the cooked apples into the colander and let the apples drip for several hours without pressing.

Makes 4 pints.

CANNING

Reheat the juice almost to the boiling point. Pour into hot, clean jars, leaving ¼ inch head space. Put on the lids and screw bands. Place the jars on a rack in a kettle of hot water deep enough to cover them by 1 inch. Bring the water to a boil and process 10 minutes. Transfer the jars to a rack or damp dishcloth and let cool with air space between the jars. Cool completely, label and store.

FREEZING

Prepare the juice as above but do not reheat. Pour into glass or plastic containers, leaving 1 inch head space. Seal, label and freeze quickly.

Quick Apple Jelly

1 pint canned or thawed frozen apple juice	1½ teaspoons bottled lemon juice
1 tablespoon powdered pectin	2½ cups sugar

Stir the juice, pectin and lemon juice over high heat in a saucepan until it comes to a full rolling boil. Add the sugar and keep stirring until it returns to the full boil. Set the timer for 1 minute. Keep stirring until the minute is over. Remove from the heat and skim off any froth with a metal spoon.

Pour into hot, clean jars, leaving ⅛ inch head space. Wipe the rims and put on lids and screw bands. Let stand for several hours until completely cooled. Label and store.

Makes 3 8-ounce jars.

Grape Juice for Jelly

6 pounds ripe Concord grapes	Water

Wash and stem the grapes, dropping them into a large saucepan or kettle. Add enough water to just barely cover the fruit. Bring to a boil. Cover and simmer 10 minutes.

Line a colander with 4 thicknesses of damp cheesecloth or an old dish towel wrung out in cool water. Suspend the juice over a bowl and let the grapes drip until dry. If time is important, press the grapes gently to press out the juice. Pour the juice into 2 quart bottles and place in the refrigerator overnight.

The next morning the grape sediment will be at the bottoms of the bottles. Decant carefully, leaving the sediment in the bottles. If necessary, pour the juice through cheesecloth before canning or freezing.

Makes 4 pints.

CANNING

Heat the juice to just below the boiling point. Pour into 4 hot, clean pint jars, leaving ¼ inch head space. Wipe the rims and adjust the lids and closures. Place the jars on a rack in a kettle of hot water deep enough to cover the jars by 1 inch. Bring to a boil and process for 5 minutes. Remove the jars and cool completely before labeling and storing.

FREEZING

Do not reheat the juice. Decant it into pint glass or plastic containers, leaving 1 inch of head space. Seal, label and freeze quickly.

Quick Grape Jelly

1 pint canned or thawed grape juice	5 teaspoons powdered pectin
	3 cups sugar

Stir the juice and powdered pectin over high heat until it comes to a full rolling boil. Add the sugar and continue stirring until the mixture boils hard. Set the timer and continue to stir for 1 minute. Remove from the heat and skim off any foam. Pour the hot jelly into hot, clean jars. Wipe off the rims. Adjust the lids and screw bands and let stand without moving for 12 hours. Label and store.

Makes 3 8-ounce jars.

Blackberry Jelly

Blackberry jelly is delicious with cream or cottage cheese. It also makes a good filling for tartlets. The following recipe will yield 1 12-ounce jar and 1 8-ounce jar. If blackberry is a favorite flavor, double the recipe and use 1 package of powdered pectin.

1	*quart blackberries*	2	*tablespoons powdered*
2	*tablespoons lemon juice*		*pectin*
		2½	*cups sugar*

Prepare your equipment and wash the jars and closures by hand (or dishwasher) so that they will be ready for filling.

Pick over the blackberries. If you are picking them yourself, choose a time shortly after a refreshing shower. Pick some red berries as well as the fully ripe blackberries. Picking the berries carefully and keeping them clean eliminates the necessity of washing them or even picking them over in the kitchen. Bought berries should be briefly washed and all stems removed.

Spin the berries in a blender or food processor or mash them with a potato masher.

Line a colander with 3 or 4 thicknesses of dampened cheesecloth or with a spotlessly clean, damp old dish towel. Suspend the colander over a stainless steel or aluminum saucepan. Let the berries drip until the pulp is dry. There should be 1¾ cups of juice. Add water or apple juice if necessary.

To the blackberry juice add the lemon juice and pectin and stir until the pectin dissolves. Place over high heat and bring to a full rolling boil. Add the sugar and stir until the mixture boils hard. Set the timer for 1 minute. Stir constantly. When the jelly has boiled for 1 minute, remove from the stove. Skim off any foam that comes to the top and pour into the prepared jars up to within ⅛ inch of the top. Put on the lids and screw bands. Let stand 12 hours before labeling and storing.

Very Special Jellies

Bar-le-Duc (Red Currant) Jelly

This jelly is named for the French city Bar-le-Duc, near which red currants grow in abundance. It is considered a great luxury and is eaten with either cream cheese or Roquefort cheese and crusty bread as a dessert.

To extract the juice: Pick or buy 1 quart of very ripe red currants. Pick them over. It is not necessary to remove the stems. Wash and drain briefly, leaving the currants quite wet. Place them either in a slow cooker (Crock Pot) or in a quart jar and then on a rack in a kettle of hot water. Cook for several hours or until the fruit is very soft and the juice is extracted.

A quicker but less traditional method of extraction is to crush the berries with a blender or food processor or with a potato masher and to simmer them with ½ cup of water for 10 minutes.

Unless you have a jelly bag and standard, line a colander with several thicknesses of cheesecloth or with a clean old dish towel. Suspend it over a bowl or stainless steel saucepan. Pour the currants and juice into the cheesecloth. Let strain until the pulp is dry. Do not squeeze.

Measure the juice and add the same amount of sugar. Stir over high heat until the mixture boils. Cook until the jelly registers 230 degrees F. on the thermometer or until quite thick. Bar-le-Duc is firmer than most jellies. Pour immediately into hot, clean jars, filling to ⅛ inch of the top. Wipe the rims. Put on the lids and screw bands tightly. Do not move the jars for 12 hours. Label and store.

Makes 2 8-ounce jars.

Buffet Ham with Bar-le-Duc Sauce

This is a wonderful party dish that can be prepared at least a day in advance. We allow ⅓ pound of ham to a person. For smaller parties or larger appetites adjust the amount of ham.

6 pounds boneless country smoked ham (precooked)	1 tablespoon grated orange rind
1 cup brown sugar	1 teaspoon grated lemon rind
¼ cup Port wine	1 cup orange juice
	1 tablespoon lemon juice
	4 teaspoons arrowroot
BAR-LE-DUC SAUCE:	2 tablespoons water
2 8-ounce jars Bar-le-Duc Jelly	¾ cup Port wine
2 tablespoons water	3 tablespoons Cointreau

Remove the strings and any excess fat from the exterior of the ham. Slice ⅛ to ¼ inch thick and lay the slices in overlapping fashion on large ovenproof serving platters or, if that is not possible, in a large roasting pan. Sprinkle with brown sugar and Port and cover with aluminum foil. Keep in a very cool place or in the refrigerator.

To make the sauce, stir the jelly and water in a saucepan over moderate heat until the jelly is melted. Add the rinds, juice and Port and simmer for 2 minutes.

Blend the arrowroot and water and stir into the sauce. As soon as the mixture starts to simmer remove from the heat. Cool and stir in the Cointreau. Let the sauce stand for at least 24 hours in the refrigerator. Serve at room temperature.

Before serving, bake the ham for 1 hour at 300 degrees F. If the party is delayed reduce the heat to 200 degrees F. and keep warm. Remove the foil and pour off any excess fat.

Garnish the platters with sprigs of parsley or watercress and serve the sauce in a separate bowl.

Serves 16 to 18 persons.

Red Pepper Jelly

This unusual jelly is sweeping the country in popularity. Spread it over a large cake of cream cheese and serve with toast or crackers at tea or cocktail time.

1	dozen red sweet peppers	1 cup white wine vinegar
1	small hot red pepper	3 cups sugar
1	tablespoon canning salt	

Wash the peppers and cut them in half. Cut out the seeds. Chop them quite fine in a food processor (or by hand) or force them through a meat grinder, using a medium coarse blade.

Place the peppers in a bowl and stir in the salt. Cover and let stand 3 hours.

Put the peppers in a colander and run cool water over them so that the salt is removed.

Place in a stainless steel or aluminum saucepan and stir in the vinegar and sugar. Bring to a boil and simmer for 25 to 30 minutes or until the thermometer registers 220 degrees F.—the jelly stage.

Pour into hot, clean jars, leaving ⅛ inch head space. Wipe the rims and put on the lids and screw bands firmly. Let the jelly stand 12 hours before moving. Label and store.

Honey Lemon Jelly

For a Sunday night supper there is nothing nicer than a plate of cold ham and hot baking-powder biscuits with butter and Honey Lemon Jelly. It bespeaks contentment.

1½	cups clover honey	⅓ cup liquid pectin
6	tablespoons lemon juice	

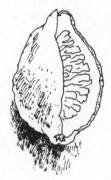

Stir the honey and lemon juice in a saucepan over high heat until it comes to a full rolling boil. Add the pectin and continue stirring until it boils hard again.

Set the timer for 1 minute and continue to stir. Remove from the heat.

Skim off any froth with a metal spoon. Pour into clean, hot glasses, filling the jars to within ⅛ inch of the top. Wipe the rims. Put on the lids and screw bands firmly. Let stand 12 hours before moving. Label and store in a dark place.

Makes 2 8-ounce glasses.

Tarragon Chablis Jelly

This jelly is particularly good served with lamb when it is cooked in the French manner—rare to medium rare.

1 cup fresh tarragon leaves	2 tablespoons powdered pectin
1¾ cups Chablis wine	1¾ cups sugar
1 tablespoon bottled lemon juice	2-3 drops green food coloring (optional)

Wash the tarragon leaves. Save out 2 or 3 leaves for each jar. Chop the rest rather coarsely in a wooden bowl.

Add the wine and stir slightly to incorporate the tarragon juices.

Pour into a stainless steel or aluminum saucepan. Bring to a boil and simmer 1 minute. Remove from the heat. Cover and steep for 15 minutes. Add food coloring, if desired.

Strain the mixture through a fine sieve into the wooden bowl. Pour the liquid back into the saucepan. Add the lemon juice and powdered pectin. Place over high heat and stir while bringing the liquid to a full rolling boil.

Set the timer for 1 minute and continue stirring.

Remove from the heat. Skim off any froth on the surface and pour into the jars, filling them to within ⅛ inch of the top. Add the reserved leaves. Wipe the rims. Cover with the lids and screw on the bands tightly. Cool for 12 hours before labeling and storing.

Makes 2 8-ounce jars.

Red Currant and Red Raspberry Jelly

There are only a few days in the year when red raspberries and red currants are ripe at the same time. Finding them is the most difficult part of this delectable jelly. If you have the space, double the recipe— but never do more than that at a time, no matter how spacious your kitchen. The long boiling required for larger amounts gives a less delicate flavor.

1 pint red raspberries	1⅛ cups sugar
1 pint red currants	

Pick over the raspberries without washing them. Place them in a saucepan and crush slightly.

Wash the currants and pick them over. Do not bother to stem.

Add the currants to the raspberries and cook covered for 10 minutes or until the currants are very soft.

Prepare a jelly bag or line a colander with several thicknesses of damp cheesecloth or with a clean old dish towel. Suspend it over a bowl or stainless steel saucepan. Let the fruit strain through the cloth until the pulp is dry.

Combine the sugar with the juice, which should measure approximately 1⅔ cups. Bring to a rapid boil, stirring constantly. Cook until the jelly registers 220 degrees F. on a thermometer or until the jelly "sheets" from the spoon. (See Apple Jelly.) Pour into hot, clean jars, filling them to within ⅛ inch of the top. Wipe the rims, put on the lids and screw bands tightly. Do not move the jelly for 12 hours. Label and store.

Makes 2 8-ounce jars.

Summer Milk Shake

1   pint milk
1   8-ounce jar raspberry-currant jelly

½   pint strawberry frozen yogurt or ice cream

Put the ingredients in a food processor, Vita-Mix, or blender and spin until blended. Serve in a long glass with a sturdy straw.

Makes 2 servings.

Rose-Hip Jelly

Rose-hip jelly is noted for its delicate flavor and pretty color as well as for its vitamin C content. The following is a simplified version of what is often a fairly complicated process.

1   cup rose hips
    (preferably wild roses)
2   cups water
4½ cups sugar

1   cup unsweetened apple
    juice (store bought)
1   package (4 tablespoons)
    powdered pectin

Remove the stem ends of the rose hips and wash them thoroughly. Place in a saucepan with 2 cups of water. Bring to a boil, cover and cook gently for 15 minutes. Mash the hips and continue cooking for 10 minutes. Pour into a nonmetal bowl and let stand covered for 24 hours.

Before cooking, prepare the jelly glasses and measure out the sugar. Strain the juice into a measuring cup. There should be 2½ cups of juice. Combine the apple juice and powdered pectin with the rose-hip juice in a large saucepan. Bring to a rapid boil, stirring over high heat. Add the sugar and continue stirring until the syrup reaches a full rolling boil. Set the timer for 1 minute and continue cooking and stirring for 1 minute.

Remove from the heat and skim off any froth on the surface. Pour into hot, clean glasses, filling the jars to within ⅛ inch of the top. Wipe the rims and adjust the closures, screwing the bands on firmly. Let the glasses stand for 12 hours. Label and store in a dark place.

Makes 5 8-ounce jars.

Jams and Conserves

You have used only strained fruit juices in making jelly; to make these jams and conserves you will be using more of the fruit pulp and even some of the peel. This means you will have to watch closely when boiling the fruit-sugar mixtures, to prevent their sticking and scorching. It will help to use a heavy-bottomed kettle rather than a thin, light-weight one.

Another difference is that for safety it will be necessary to process these jars in a hot-water-bath canner, as in canning fruit—a step that can be skipped when you make jelly.

Blueberry Conserve

For a delicious dessert make or buy individual tart shells and fill them with this conserve. Cover with a thick sauce made from cream cheese softened with a very little milk.

1 quart blueberries	1 cup seeded raisins
1 orange	4 cups sugar
1 lemon	½ cup chopped walnuts

Pick over the blueberries and wash them. Place in a flat-bottomed saucepan and mash them slightly.

Cut the orange and lemon into wedges and remove the seeds and coarse fibers. Force the orange, lemon and raisins through a meat grinder or chop them in a food processor. Add the fruit and sugar to the blueberries and cook until thick or until the mixture measures 220 degrees F. on the thermometer. Remove from the heat and cool. Stir in the chopped walnuts. Fill clean jars to within ¼ inch of the top. Wipe the rims and adjust the lids and screw bands. Place on a rack in a kettle of hot water so that the jars are covered by 1 inch. Bring to a boil and process 10 minutes. Remove to a rack or damp towel to cool completely before labeling and storing.

Makes 3 8-ounce jars.

Cantaloupe and Peach Jam

4 peaches	1 teaspoon grated lemon peel
½ teaspoon crystalline	4 teaspoons powdered pectin
ascorbic acid	1⅓ cups sugar
1 cup diced cantaloupe	

Dip the peaches in boiling water for 30 seconds (two at a time). Place them immediately in cold water. Halve them and remove the skins, the pits and the pink fibrous centers. Cut into very small pieces into a bowl. Stir in the ascorbic acid.

Cut the cantaloupe into equally small pieces. Add them to the peaches along with the grated lemon peel and powdered pectin.

Stir well and put into a saucepan. Bring to a rapid boil. Add the sugar and stir until it again reaches a full boil. Set the timer for 1 minute. Continue stirring until the minute is up.

Remove the jam from the heat and continue stirring for several minutes, skimming off any froth that rises to the surface. Pour into hot, clean glasses. Wipe the rims. Adjust the lids and screw the bands on firmly. Cool completely before labeling and storing.

Makes 2 8-ounce jars.

Gooseberry Jam

The native American gooseberry is purplish blue and grows wild in many parts of the country. The hybridized cultivated variety brought from England is yellow or yellow green. The flavors of both varieties are strikingly similar and they can be prepared the same way. Gooseberry jam is lovely on scones or English muffins. It can also be quickly transformed into frozen Gooseberry Fool, which is a dinner-party dessert.

5 cups gooseberries	½ cup water
1 tablespoon grated orange rind	2 tablespoons powdered pectin
	3½ cups sugar

Wash the gooseberries. Measure out 1 cup and remove the stem and blossom ends.

Put the rest of the gooseberries through a meat grinder, saving all the juice, or spin in a food processor. Force through a food mill.

Combine the strained gooseberries with the orange rind, water, powdered pectin and the stemmed gooseberries in a large saucepan.

Stir over high heat until the mixture comes to a full boil. Add the sugar and continue stirring until the mixture boils hard. Set the timer for 1 minute and continue stirring until the minute is up. Remove from the heat and continue stirring for 5 minutes, removing any froth that comes to the surface.

Pour into hot, clean glasses, leaving ½ inch head space. Adjust the lids and closures and let the jam cool completely before labeling and storing.

Makes 4 8-ounce jars.

Frozen Gooseberry Fool

2   8-ounce jars gooseberry jam   1   teaspoon vanilla
1   pint whipping cream

Whisk the jam for a moment.

Beat the cream until stiff and add the vanilla. Fold the whipped cream into the jam. Pour into a slightly moistened 1-quart mold and cover with 2 sheets of aluminum foil. Let stand in the freezer for several hours.

Unmold onto a dessert platter.

Serves 6 to 8 persons.

Fresh Mango Chutney

Mangoes are becoming so common in the supermarket that it is no longer necessary to fake the real thing with watermelon rind or green tomatoes. Chill before serving with curries or roasts.

1   cup white sugar   1   cup peeled and chopped
1   cup brown sugar   peaches
1½ cups cider vinegar   ⅛   teaspoon chili powder
¾   cup seeded raisins   ¼   teaspoon salt
4   tablespoons chopped onion   ¼   teaspoon cinnamon
⅔   cup chopped candied ginger   ⅛   teaspoon nutmeg
3   cups peeled and chopped
    mangoes

Combine everything in a kettle and stir until the mixture boils. Cook over moderate heat until the mixture is thick and measures 215 degrees F. on the thermometer.

Fill hot, clean jars within ⅛ inch of the top of the jars. Wipe the rims and put on the lids and screw bands firmly. Process 10 minutes in the boiling water bath. Cool, label and store.

Makes 3 8-ounce jars.

Seville-Like Orange Marmalade

Marmalade made from Seville oranges is considered the best in the world. This simple recipe approximates the flavor, and the trick seems to be in overcooking it a little. The recipe makes a lot, so if marmalade is a daily ritual in your home save space by packing some of it in pint jars and the rest in ½ pints. Once opened, it will keep almost indefinitely in the refrigerator. Keep it covered.

1 *thin-skinned orange*	1 *thin-skinned grapefruit*
1 *thin-skinned lemon*	*Sugar*

Wash the fruit very thoroughly. Using a sharp knife, cut as thinly as possible, removing the seeds and cores. To cut in a food processor, divide each fruit into sections, removing the core and seeds. Force them through the food slicer. Be careful to save the juice.

Measure the fruit and juice into a kettle. For every cup add 3 cups of water. Bring to a boil, cover and simmer 1½ hours. Remove from the heat and let stand 12 hours.

Divide the mixture between 2 large saucepans, measuring it in the process. For every cup add 1 cup of sugar. Bring to a boil, stirring frequently. Cook until the syrup is thick and fairly dark or until it measures 226 degrees F. on the thermometer (a little past the jelly stage). This can take as long as an hour.

Pour the marmalade into the kettle and let stand until almost cool, stirring frequently to distribute the fruit. Pour into clean pint or ½ pint jars and put on the lids and screw bands.

For perfect sealing, process in a boiling water bath for 10 minutes.

Remove from hot water and let stand on a rack or towel until cool, then label and store.

Makes 72 ounces.

Quick Spiced Peach Jam

This jam takes 25 to 30 minutes to make.

2 tablespoons water	½ teaspoon cinnamon
2 tablespoons lemon juice	4 cups cut-up peaches
¼ teaspoon cloves	3 cups sugar

Combine the water, lemon juice, cloves and cinnamon in a quart saucepan.

Dip the peaches in boiling water for 30 seconds and rinse in cold water. Peel and cut in small pieces into a measuring cup. Add them a cupful at a time to the saucepan, giving them a quick stir. When all the peaches are in the saucepan, bring to a boil and cook until soft, stirring frequently. This should take 6 to 8 minutes.

Stirring with one hand, add the sugar with the other. Stir over moderate heat until the mixture boils. Increase the heat and cook until the mixture thickens or measures 220 degrees F. on the thermometer.

Pour into hot, clean jars, leaving ¼ inch head space. Wipe the rims and put on the lids and screw bands very firmly, then process in a boiling water bath for 10 minutes. Cool, label and store in a dark place.

Makes 4 8-ounce jars.

Brandied Pear Butter

This is delicious spread on toast and served with a cup of tea. It has a very special flavor.

10 ripe pears	¼ teaspoon mace
2 cups sugar	4 tablespoons apricot, peach or
½ teaspoon ground ginger	pear brandy
1 teaspoon grated lemon rind	

Wash, stem, peel and core the pears. Spin them to a puree in a blender, doing 3 or 4 pears at a time. You should have 4 cups of puree.

Place the puree in a saucepan with the sugar, lemon rind, ginger and mace. Bring to a boil and cook 15 minutes or until very thick. Add the brandy and cook 5 minutes longer. Do not let the mixture burn.

Pour into hot, clean jars to within ¼ inch of the top. Wipe the rims and put on the lids. Screw the bands on firmly. Place the jars on a rack in a kettle and cover them with hot water. Bring to a boil and process for 10 minutes. The water in the kettle should be deep enough to cover the jar tops by 1 inch.

Withdraw the jars and set them on a rack or damp towel to cool completely before labeling and storing.

Makes 2 8-ounce jars.

Old-Fashioned Pumpkin Chip Jam

Not all pumpkins have to go into pies or be made into jack-o'-lanterns. Here is a recipe our American foremothers used to make.

4 cups sliced pumpkin	Grated rind and juice of
2 cups sugar	½ orange
1 lemon, sliced thin	4 tablespoons finely diced, crystallized ginger

Wash a small pumpkin and cut it into eighths. Remove the seeds and peel off the skin. Using a very sharp knife or food processor, slice the pumpkin very thin.

Combine the pumpkin chips with the sugar, the sliced and seeded lemon, the orange rind and juice and the ginger. Stir over moderate heat until the mixture boils. Continue cooking slowly for 10 to 15 minutes or until the pumpkin is shiny and translucent.

Pour into hot, clean jars, leaving ¼ inch head space. Wipe the rims and adjust the lids. Put on the screw bands very firmly, then process the jam for 10 minutes in a boiling water bath.

Cool, label and store.

Makes 3 8-ounce jars.

Strawberry Jam

1 quart wild or garden strawberries	3 cups sugar
	2 teaspoons lemon juice

Wash the berries as briefly as possible. Remove the hulls and throw the berries into an enamel-lined or stainless steel pan.

Add the sugar and crush the berries slightly to bring out some of the juice. Bring to a boil and cook 15 to 20 minutes or until thick. Add the lemon juice and boil 1 minute.

Ladle the jam into the jars, leaving ¼ inch head space. Adjust lids and closures. Process 15 minutes in a boiling water bath. Let cool before storing.

Makes 4 8-ounce jars.

Strawberry-Jam Roll

4 egg yolks	2 8-ounce jars strawberry jam
12 tablespoons fine sugar	1 cup heavy cream, whipped
¾ cup sifted cake flour	2 tablespoons sifted
1 teaspoon baking powder	confectioners'
⅓ teaspoon salt	sugar (optional)
½ teaspoon almond extract	½ teaspoon vanilla extract
4 egg whites, beaten stiff	(optional)

Prepare the jelly-roll pan: line a 10-inch by 15-inch rimmed baking sheet with wax paper and brush it lightly with oil or melted butter.

Preheat the oven to 375 degrees F.

Beat the egg yolks until pale yellow. Still beating, add the sugar tablespoonful by tablespoonful until the mixture is pale and creamy.

Combine and sift the dry ingredients. Add them to the egg yolk mixture and stir until thoroughly blended.

Stir in the almond extract and fold in the beaten egg whites thoroughly but gently.

Pour the mixture into the prepared pan and smooth it evenly with a spatula. Bake 12 minutes or until the cake springs back when pressed with your finger.

While the cake is baking, spread a slightly dampened, spotlessly clean kitchen towel on a working surface. Sprinkle it with sieved confectioners' sugar. Turn the cake upside down on the towel. If the edges are crisp, cut them off (with the paper) with a long sharp knife. If not, just peel off the wax paper. While the cake is still hot, roll the cake up with the help of the towel and let it cool under the towel.

Gently unroll the cake and spread the inside with 1½ cups of the strawberry jam. Reroll it and place it on a long serving tray. Spread the surface with the whipped cream and decorate the top with the remaining ½ cup of jam.

Serves 6 to 8 persons.

Rhubarb Conserve

Buy or gather thin red stalks of rhubarb for this conserve. They are sweeter than the green stalks and make a prettier conserve.

1 *pound rhubarb stalks*	1½ *cups sugar*
½ *cup water*	3 *tablespoons chopped,*
1 *stick (2 inches) cinnamon*	*crystallized ginger*
1 *pint strawberries*	½ *cup chopped walnuts*

Wash the rhubarb stalks and cut them into ½-inch pieces. Place in a saucepan. Add the water. Break up the cinnamon stick and put it in a stainless steel tea ball or tie it in a small muslin bag. Put it in the saucepan and bring the rhubarb to a boil. Reduce the heat and simmer for 20 minutes or until the rhubarb is very soft.

Meanwhile, wash the strawberries. Hull them and spin them in a blender or food processor.

When the rhubarb is soft, withdraw the tea ball and add the strawberries, sugar, ginger and nuts. Increase the heat and boil for 15 to 20 minutes or until the jelly stage has been reached (220 degrees F.). Remove from the heat and stir gently, removing any froth that gathers on the surface. Let the jam cool for 10 minutes, stirring every 2 or 3 minutes.

Pour into hot, clean jars, filling to within ¼ inch of the top. Wipe the rims and adjust the lids and closures, screwing the bands on very tightly. Process 15 minutes in a boiling water bath. Let cool completely before labeling and storing.

Makes 3 8-ounce jars.

'Tis or 'Taint Apple Butter

" 'Tis" apple butter is fortified with brandy. " 'Taint" is for those who prefer not to indulge. Either way, this butter is delicious spread on toast or English muffins and makes a wonderful dessert when spread between layers of cake, which are then frosted with sweet whipped cream.

10-12	medium (3 pounds) cooking apples	¼	teaspoon ground cloves
1	cup water	¼	teaspoon salt
1	pint sweet cider	1	teaspoon lemon juice
1½	cups light brown sugar	½	cup Calvados or applejack (optional)
1	teaspoon cinnamon		

Stem and wash the apples. Cut into pieces without coring or peeling them and put in a saucepan with 1 cup of water. Cover and bring to a boil. Remove the cover and cook 15 to 20 minutes or until soft. Stir occasionally.

Meanwhile, pour the cider into a heavy 3-quart pan or kettle and boil it down to half its original quantity. Remove from the heat and stir in the sugar, cinnamon, cloves and salt.

Place a food mill or sieve over the kettle and press the apples into the cider mixture. Place the kettle over high heat and stir for 10 minutes or until the sauce begins to thicken. Reduce the heat to moderate and cook for about an hour, stirring frequently to prevent scorching. The mixture should be very thick. Remove from the heat and stir in the lemon juice and, for those who want "'Tis," stir in the apple brandy. Pour into hot, clean jars, leaving ¼ inch head space. Put on the lids and screw the bands on tightly.

Rinse out the kettle and put in a trivet or wire rack, then fill with boiling water. Lower the jars into the water and bring to a boil. The jars should be covered by at least 1 inch. Process 10 minutes. Remove the jars and cool completely before labeling and storing.

Makes 4 8-ounce jars.

Apple Butter Dessert Cake

1 cup sifted cake flour	1 8-ounce jar apple butter
1 teaspoon baking powder	½ pint heavy cream
¼ teaspoon salt	4 tablespoons sifted confec-
1 medium-size lemon	tioners' sugar
2 eggs	1 teaspoon vanilla extract
1 cup fine sugar	Candied violets (optional)
6 tablespoons hot water	

Preheat the oven to 350 degrees F. Spray 2 8-inch layer cake tins with nonstick coating.

Sift the flour, baking powder and salt together and set aside. Grate the rind of the lemon and squeeze the juice.

Separate the eggs between two mixing bowls. Beat the egg whites until stiff but still moist. Set aside. Beat the egg yolks for 30 seconds. Start adding the sugar gradually and beat until pale yellow. Beat in the hot water, the lemon rind and 1 tablespoon lemon juice. Reduce the beater to its lowest speed and beat in the flour. Remove the beater and fold in the egg whites gently with a spatula. Divide the batter between the prepared baking tins and bake 25 minutes.

Turn the cakes onto wire racks and cool completely.

Spread a thick layer of the apple butter between the layers and spread a thin layer on the top.

Whip the cream until stiff and flavor it with the sugar and vanilla. Frost the top and sides. If you want to be fancy, decorate the top and sides with more whipped cream, using a decorative pastry tube or "comb" the top with concentric circles if you happen to have the special gadget. Garnish with the candied violets or with pecan halves. Keep in the refrigerator until just before serving.

This dessert can be made a week or two in advance and kept in the freezer. Allow the cake to freeze uncovered before wrapping it. Unwrap it as you take it from the freezer. Allow 1 hour to thaw.

Serves 8 persons.

Sherry Ginger Pear Sauce

This is a version of pear butter, but we like it best served on lemon sherbet or vanilla ice cream or with yogurt. It takes very little time to make.

2 pounds (5-6) Bartlett or Bosc pears	1 teaspoon grated lemon rind
1½ cups sugar	⅛ teaspoon cinnamon
2 teaspoons lemon juice	⅛ teaspoon ground cloves
4 tablespoons sherry	3 tablespoons chopped candied ginger
1 teaspoon grated orange rind	

Peel and core the pears. If they are underripe and hard, cut them in pieces and boil until soft. If ripe, force them uncooked through a food mill or puree them in a food processor.

Place the pears in a heavy saucepan with the rest of the ingredients. Bring to a boil and cook gently for 15 minutes or until very thick. Pour into the jars, leaving ¼ inch head space. Adjust the lids and put on the screw bands.

Place the jars on a rack in a pan of boiling water deep enough to cover the jars by 1 inch. Bring to a boil and process 10 minutes. Remove from the water to cool completely before labeling and storing.

Makes 2 8-ounce jars.

No-Sugar Jellies and Jams

No-sugar jellies and jams bought in the market are an expensive luxury, but they can easily be made at home. Most no-sugar preserves have to be kept in precious refrigerator or freezer space, so it is best to make them in small jars and in very small batches. A note of warning: There is a strange, unpleasant odor when fruit and artificial sweetener are boiling. This disappears when they cool-and does not affect the taste.

No-Sugar Apple Jelly

Using the principle of making repeated batches of apple and grape jelly from canned or frozen juice (page 92), make 2 glasses of jelly at a time. It takes no time to make it. All you need for equipment is 2 hot, clean jelly jars and a small saucepan.

2 *cups apple juice*	3 *teaspoons liquid artificial*
2 *teaspoons lemon juice*	*sweetener*
1 *package (1 tablespoon)*	2-4 *drops red vegetable coloring*
unflavored gelatin	

Mix the apple juice, lemon juice and gelatin softened in water in a small saucepan. Bring to a rapid boil over high heat, stirring. Boil 1 minute and remove from the heat. Stir in the sweetener and coloring and pour into hot, clean jars. Wipe the rims and adjust the lids and closures. Cool, label and store in the refrigerator. Always keep covered after opening and do not let the jelly stand too long, once opened. It loses flavor and texture.

Makes 2 8-ounce jars.

VARIATIONS

No-Sugar Apple Mint: Follow the above directions. After removing the juice from the heat, swirl several sprays of well-washed mint leaves in it before adding the sweetener and a few drops of green vegetable coloring.

No-Sugar Cinnamon Jelly: Add 1 teaspoon of powdered cinnamon to the jelly before boiling. Color the jelly bright red. This will hide any flecks of cinnamon.

No-Sugar Cranberry Jelly

1 pint low-calorie store-bought
  cranberry juice
1 package (tablespoon)
  unflavored gelatin

1 tablespoon water
2 teaspoons grated orange rind
1 tablespoon liquid
  artificial sweetener

Combine in a saucepan the cranberry juice with the gelatin softened in water and the orange rind. Bring to a boil over high heat, stirring. Boil 1 minute. Remove from the heat and add the sweetener. Pour into hot, clean jars. Wipe the rims. Adjust the lids and screw bands. Cool completely and then store in the refrigerator.

For special occasions, double the recipe. Add 1 cup of seedless grapes and pour into a quart ring mold. Cool, cover and let set in the refrigerator for several hours. Unmold on a bed of lettuce. Garnish with orange slices and white grapes and serve with regular or low-calorie mayonnaise.

Makes 2 8-ounce jars.

No-Sugar Grape Jelly

If you are extracting the juice, allow 1 very full quart of grapes for 1½ cups of juice. (See page 99.) For repeated batches follow the suggestions for canning or freezing grape juice on page 100.

1½ cups unsweetened grape juice
2 packages (tablespoons)
  unflavored gelatin
2 tablespoons water

4 teaspoons lemon juice
2 tablespoons artificial
  liquid sweetener

Bring the grape juice, the gelatin softened in water and the lemon juice to a full rolling boil, stirring constantly. Boil 1 minute. Remove from the heat and stir in the sweetener. Pour into hot, clean jars. Wipe the rims and adjust the lids and closures. Cool, label and store in the refrigerator. Once a jar is opened, keep the unused portion tightly covered. Do not keep longer than 1 week.

Makes 2 8-ounce jars.

Spiced Concord Grape Jelly

1½   cups Concord grape juice
½   teaspoon powdered cinnamon
½   teaspoon powdered cloves
3   tablespoons vinegar (cider or wine)

2   packages (tablespoons) unflavored gelatin
2   tablespoons water
2   tablespoons liquid artificial sweetener

Combine the grape juice, cinnamon, cloves, vinegar and gelatin, softened in water in a saucepan, and bring to a rapid boil over high heat. Stir in the sweetener and pour into hot, clean jars. Wipe the rims and adjust the lids and closures. Cool, label and store in the refrigerator. Once a jar is opened, keep it covered in the refrigerator and use it within 1 week.

No-Sugar Frozen Spiced Peach Jam

2   pounds peaches
1   medium-size tart apple
½   teaspoon ascorbic acid
1   teaspoon grated orange rind
2   tablespoons orange juice
½   teaspoon allspice

½   teaspoon powdered cloves
½   teaspoon cinnamon
1   tablespoon artificial liquid sweetener
1   package powdered pectin

Dip the peaches in boiling water, 2 by 2, for 30 seconds. Place immediately in cold water. Peel the peaches and cut them into sections into a bowl. Crush slightly. Sprinkle with the ascorbic acid and stir. Peel and core the apple and dice coarsely.

Add the apple, orange rind, juice, spices and the sweetener to the peaches. Mix well and place in a small saucepan. Bring the mixture to a rapid boil, stirring. Cook for 2 minutes.

Remove from the heat and keep stirring for a few moments to keep the fruit from settling. Pour into hot, clean freezing jars, leaving ¼ inch head space. Adjust the lids and closures. Cool and place in the freezer. Once a jar is opened, keep the unused jam covered in the refrigerator.

Makes 2 8-ounce jars.

No-Sugar Raspberry, Blackberry or Strawberry Jam

1   quart ripe berries
1   tablespoon lemon juice

½   cup liquid artificial
      sweetener

Pick over the berries and place them in a saucepan. Crush them with a potato masher and stir in the lemon juice and sweetener. Bring to a boil over high heat and continue to stir until the mixture becomes quite thick.

Pour the jam into hot, clean glasses, leaving ¼ inch head space. Wipe the rims. Adjust the lids and closures, screwing the bands on tightly. Place the jars on a rack in a deep saucepan full of enough hot water to cover the jars by 1 inch. Bring the water to a boil and boil 15 minutes. Remove from the water and let cool completely before labeling and storing. This requires no refrigeration until the jar is opened.

Makes 2 8-ounce jars.

Pickles
and Relishes

Making pickles is like eating peanuts. You always want to make a little bit more because it is so easy, so inexpensive and so wonderful to smell while they are cooking. Our advice is not only to make pickles in small batches but also in small jars. A large jar of pickles or relish is often half used at a meal and then pushed to the back of the refrigerator abandoned and forgotten.

If you are tempted to make more than you need, remember pickles make much-appreciated hostess or Christmas gifts and they always sell well at the church bazaar. Variety, rather than quantity, makes pickle making and pickle eating a very pleasant occupation.

Old-Fashioned Bread and Butter Pickles

3 cups sliced cucumbers	½ cup vinegar
1 cup small green pepper slices	½ cup sugar
2 cups small white onions, sliced	1½ teaspoons turmeric
	1½ teaspoons mustard seed
2 tablespoons canning salt	1½ teaspoons celery seed

Put the prepared vegetables in a nonmetal bowl. Stir in the canning salt. Cover and let stand 2 to 3 hours.

Combine the vinegar, sugar and spices in a saucepan. Bring to a boil.

Drain the vegetables well and add them to the saucepan. Boil 5 minutes. Pour into hot, clean jars, filling to within ½ inch of the top. Wipe the rims and put on the lids and screw bands. Place them on a rack in a kettle of water deep enough to cover the jars by 1 inch. Bring to a boil and process 5 minutes. Remove the jars and let cool on a rack or damp dish towel before labeling and storing.

Makes 2 pints or 4 ½-pint jars.

Morning and Evening Sweet Gherkin Pickles

This recipe is only for those who have a corner on the counter where they can leave a large bowl for four days. By administering briefly to the pickles for that length of time—both morning and evening—you will achieve delicious pickles.

2½-3 pounds tiny cucumbers (2-3 inches long)
    Boiling water
4 tablespoons canning salt
3 cups vinegar
4 cups sugar
½ teaspoon (scant) turmeric
1 teaspoon celery seed
1 teaspoon mixed pickling spice
1 4-inch piece cinnamon stick
1 clove garlic

On the first morning, scrub and wash the cucumbers, leaving a little of the stem end of each cucumber. Place in a nonmetal bowl and cover with boiling water.

That evening drain off the boiling water and cover with more boiling water.

The next morning drain and cover with boiling water again.

That evening drain and cover with boiling water, adding the canning salt.

The next morning drain the cucumbers in a colander and rinse out the bowl. Prick each cucumber with the tines of a fork and put back into the bowl. Combine half the sugar and half the vinegar in a small saucepan with the turmeric and seeds. Put the cinnamon stick, broken into pieces, and the garlic, peeled and halved, into a stainless steel tea ball and place in the saucepan. Bring the mixture to a boil and pour over the cucumbers, tea ball and all.

That evening drain off the syrup into a saucepan. Add the tea ball and the remaining sugar and vinegar. Bring to a boil and pour over the pickles.

The next morning drain off the syrup. Bring to a boil with the tea ball. Remove the tea ball and pour the syrup over the cucumbers.

That evening, pour off the syrup into a saucepan. Pack the cucumbers into clean, hot jars, filling them to within ¾ inch of the top. Bring the syrup to a full boil and pour into the jars, filling them to within ½ inch of the top. Put on the lids and the screw bands. Place on a rack in a kettle of hot water deep enough to cover the jars by 1 inch. Bring to a boil and process 5 minutes. Set jars on a rack to cool, leaving air space in between. When they are thoroughly cool, label and store.

Makes 4 pints.

Quick Cucumber Pickles

4 cups chopped cucumbers	¼ teaspoon turmeric
2 cups chopped onions	1 cup cider vinegar
1 green pepper, chopped	¼ teaspoon mustard seed
1 red pepper, chopped	¼ teaspoon celery seed
2 teaspoons canning salt	½ cup sugar

Wash the cucumbers and chop them rather coarsely by hand or in a food processor. Place in a bowl.

Chop the onions and add them to the cucumbers.

Wash the peppers. Halve them and remove the seeds and membranes.

Chop coarsely. Add them to the other vegetables. Sprinkle with salt and stir for 2 or 3 minutes.

Line a colander with 3 thicknesses of damp cheesecloth and drain the vegetables for 15 minutes.

Combine the turmeric, vinegar, seeds and sugar. Bring to a boil in a deep saucepan. Add the drained vegetables and bring to a boil. Simmer 5 minutes.

Pack in hot, clean jars to within ½ inch of the top. Wipe the rims and put on the lids and screw bands very tightly. Place on a rack in enough hot water to cover the tops of the jars by at least 1 inch. Cover and quickly bring the water to a boil. Set the timer for 5 minutes, and process until the time is up.

Remove the jars from the water to a rack or damp towel. Cool completely before labeling and storing in a dark place.

Makes 4 pints.

Green and Yellow Dilly Beans

There comes a time in mid to late August when everyone has too many beans in his garden and is only too willing to share. A mere pound of beans will make 4 convenient jars that will serve as delicious low-calorie appetizers or, when served with lettuce and sliced red onion, a good salad. The only reason for combining the beans is that they look so pretty both in and out of the jars.

1 pound green and yellow beans	½ teaspoon celery seed
2 cloves garlic	½ cup cider vinegar
2 heads dill	½ cup water
½ teaspoon mustard seed	2 tablespoons salt

Wash the beans, trim the ends and cut them evenly ½ inch shorter than the height of the jars. Holding a jar at a tilt, take the time to alternate green and yellow beans around the sides of the jar. Pack the beans in the center as closely together as possible without breaking them. Insert a half clove of peeled garlic and a half head of dill in each jar.

Combine the seeds, vinegar, water and salt in a saucepan and bring to a boil. Place the jars in a pan of hot water and pour the brine into the jars, leaving ¼ inch head space. Insert a plastic or wooden knife into each jar to release air bubbles. Put on the lids and screw bands.

Place the jars on a rack in a pan of hot water deep enough to cover the jars by at least 1 inch. Bring to a boil and process 10 minutes.

Remove the jars to a rack or damp towel and let cool completely before labeling and storing.

Makes 4 8-ounce jars.

Lucille's Green Tomato Pickle

These pickles are crisp and delicious. Calcium hydroxide (slaked lime) is available at any drugstore.

2 pounds green tomatoes	¼ teaspoon powdered cloves
9 cups water	¼ teaspoon ginger
3 teaspoons calcium hydroxide (slaked lime)	¼ teaspoon allspice
	¼ teaspoon celery seed
3 cups sugar	¼ teaspoon mace
1¾ cups cider vinegar	¼ teaspoon cinnamon

Choose small green tomatoes not much larger than a golf ball. Slice them thin, after washing.

Combine the water and calcium hydroxide in a bowl. Add the tomatoes and let them stand for 24 hours.

Drain and soak in fresh, cold water for 4 hours, changing the water every 30 minutes. Drain thoroughly.

Bring the sugar, vinegar and spices to a boil in a saucepan. Add the tomatoes and let stand overnight. Add a few drops of green vegetable coloring and boil 45 to 60 minutes or until the tomatoes are lustrous and clear.

Pour into hot, clean jars, leaving ½ inch head space. Wipe the rims, put on the lids and screw on the bands tightly. Cool completely before labeling and storing.

Makes 3 8-ounce jars.

Zucchini Pickles

4 cups sliced zucchini	1 cup cider vinegar
½ cup sliced onion	¼ teaspoon turmeric
2 tablespoons canning salt	¾ teaspoon mustard seed
1 cup brown sugar	¼ teaspoon celery seed

Wash the zucchini well before slicing. Combine the vegetables in a wooden bowl and sprinkle with the salt. Cover with ice water and ice cubes. Let stand for 3 hours, adding ice cubes occasionally.

Combine the sugar, vinegar, turmeric and seeds and bring to a boil.

Drain the vegetables and put them in the syrup. Heat to the simmering point but do not boil.

Pour the pickles into hot, clean jars, leaving ¼ inch head room. Adjust the lids and closures and place on a rack in a kettle of hot water deep enough to cover the jars by at least 1 inch. Bring to a boil and process for 10 minutes.

Remove from the water and cool completely on a rack before labeling and storing in a dark, cool place.

Makes 2 pints.

Whole Green Tomato Pickle — Kosher Style

For a lovely light lunch or perhaps a midnight snack, spread a slice of dark rye or pumpernickel bread with sweet butter. Cover with a slice of baked or boiled ham and slices of these pickles. A glass of cold beer completes the picture.

1 *pound small green tomatoes*	1½ *tablespoons canning salt*
2 *sprigs dill*	1 *teaspoon pickling spices*
½ *cup cider vinegar*	2 *cloves garlic*
1½ *cups water*	

Wash and dry the tomatoes. Put as many as possible into clean jars. Put a peeled garlic clove and a sprig of washed dill in each jar.

Combine the vinegar, water, canning salt and the spices contained in a stainless steel tea ball or in a small muslin bag. Bring the mixture to a boil. Cover and simmer 10 minutes. Withdraw the tea ball or muslin bag and pour the boiling brine into the jars, leaving ½ inch head space. Adjust the seals and screw bands.

Put the jars on a rack in a kettle of hot water deep enough to cover the jar tops by 1 inch. Bring to a boil and process for 15 minutes.

Remove the jars to a rack or damp towel and cool completely before labeling and storing.

Makes 2 pints.

Honeyed Watermelon Pickle

When watermelon is on the menu, it's a shame not to use the rind occasionally for making watermelon pickles. This is easily done in small quantities.

2 *cups prepared watermelon rind*	½ *cup white wine vinegar*
2 *tablespoons canning salt*	½ *lemon, sliced thin and seeded*
½ *cup clover honey*	½ *stick cinnamon*
½ *cup sugar*	1 *teaspoon whole cloves*

Trim any remaining pink flesh from the rind and pare the skin.

Cut into slices ¾ inch thick. Place in a nonmetal bowl and sprinkle with salt. Stir for a moment. Cover and let stand for 4 to 6 hours.

Drain the watermelon and run cold water through it to remove the salt.

Place in a saucepan and add enough water to barely cover. Bring to a boil and cook until just tender. Pour off all but approximately 1/2 cup of the water.

Add the honey, sugar, vinegar, lemon slices and the cinnamon and cloves encased in a stainless steel tea ball or small muslin bag.

Stir until the mixture boils. Cook gently uncovered until the rind is transparent and shiny. Remove the spices and pack in hot, clean jars, leaving ¼ inch head room. Adjust the lids and closures (after wiping the rims) and screw the bands firmly. Cool completely before labeling and storing.

Makes 2 8-ounce jars.

Pickled Mushrooms

Pickled mushrooms make an appetizing hors d'oeuvre or a nice salad component. If mushrooms are in season, you may want to double or triple the recipe.

1 12-ounce package button mushrooms	1 bay leaf
1 cup white vinegar	2 cloves
1 cup water	4 peppercorns
½ teaspoon salt	3 tablespoons olive oil
1 clove garlic, peeled and sliced	3 tablespoons tarragon vinegar

Wash the small mushrooms briefly in hot water and cut off the ends of the stems if soiled or bruised. Rinse in cold water.

Put the water, white vinegar and salt in a small saucepan. Enclose the garlic, bay leaf, cloves and peppercorns in a stainless steel tea ball or in a small muslin bag and drop it into the pan. Bring the liquid to a boil over slow heat. Cover and simmer 5 minutes. Add the mushrooms to the liquid, which should just cover them. Boil 5 minutes.

Remove from the heat. Cover and let stand 15 minutes. Remove the tea ball or muslin bag. Drain the mushrooms.

Put the olive oil and tarragon vinegar in a hot, clean jar. Add the mushrooms, poking them down with a wooden or plastic spoon which has been dipped in boiling water. Leave ½ inch head space. Put on the lid and screw band. Place on a rack in a pan of boiling water with enough water to cover the jar by 1 inch. Boil 10 minutes. Remove and cool completely before labeling and storing.

Makes 1 8-ounce jar.

Shortcuts and Standbys

Frozen Standbys

Frozen Standbys is a term for convenient items that can be prepared at a leisure moment and packed away in the freezer for those times when there is no leisure but when meals must be prepared.

Included in this list are chopped onions, chopped peppers—both green and red—buttered mushrooms (duxelles) and Cream Sauce. Packaged in small quantities, they take up very little room in the freezer and are a great source of comfort and culinary confidence on occasion.

Chopped Onions

When onions are abundant and there is space still to spare in the freezer, chop a cupful of onions. Spread them on a small baking sheet and place in the coldest part of the freezer. After the onions are frozen, pack them in ¼-, ½-, or 1-pint containers. They will stay separated so that you can take out what you want to use by the tablespoonful. After you use some of the onions, fill the vacated place with a little crumpled wax paper before resealing.

Green Peppers

Remove all seeds and white membranes from green (or red) peppers. Chop the peppers, then freeze and package like Chopped Onions. Green and red peppers can be packaged separately or together.

Mushrooms

Do not wash the mushrooms. Clean with a small bristle or goose-feather brush and trim the stem ends. Slice the caps and stems together or chop coarsely. Freeze and package like Chopped Onions.

Chopped Mushrooms in Butter (Duxelles)

Wash and trim 1 pound of firm, fresh mushrooms. Dry well and chop fine. If using a food processor, chop no more than 10 mushrooms at a time. Place the chopped mushrooms on a clean kitchen towel. Twist the towel around the mushrooms and squeeze out all the moisture into a bowl. (The juice can be used in soups, sauces or gravies. Combine it with hot homemade chicken broth and top it with a little salted whipped cream and you have a soup fit for the gods.) To continue with the mushrooms in your towel:

Heat 6 tablespoons of butter in a skillet. Sauté the mushrooms over low heat, stirring occasionally with a fork until all the moisture has disappeared. Cool. Pack in ¼- and ½-pint containers, leaving ½ inch head room. Seal, label and freeze.

Use for stuffing poultry or fish, for making bisques, soufflés and sauces or for spreading on rounds of toast to be served hot as a canapé or as a first course for a dinner party.

Cream Sauce and Variations

Cream Sauce

Cream Sauce is very helpful to have on hand. The following recipe for 1 pint can be doubled or quadrupled. Pack the sauce in ½-pint and pint containers, leaving ½ inch head space. Before serving, reheat the sauce in a double boiler, whisking well, and taste for seasoning since freezing seems to dull spices somewhat.

4 tablespoons butter or margarine	2 cups milk
4 tablespoons unbleached white or whole wheat pastry flour	Salt and pepper

Heat the butter or margarine over moderate heat. Whisk in the flour and cook over low heat for 2 minutes without letting it brown. Whisk in the milk and continue whisking until smooth and thick. Season to taste with salt and pepper. (For thicker Cream Sauce, increase the amounts of butter or margarine and flour to 6 tablespoons.) Cool, then chill and freeze.

Mornay (Cheese) Sauce

Serve with chicken, fish, egg, vegetable and some meat dishes.

1 pint Cream Sauce	1 teaspoon Dijon mustard
½ cup medium sharp Cheddar cheese or ¼ cup grated Gruyère plus ¼ cup freshly grated Parmesan	1 egg yolk (later addition)

To the Cream Sauce add the cheese of your choice and the mustard.

Stir until thoroughly blended. Pour into the freezer container leaving ½ inch head space. Chill, label and freeze.

Reheat in a double boiler. Stir in the beaten egg yolk very gradually, whisking constantly. Taste for seasoning.

Mustard Sauce

Serve with meat and egg dishes.

1 pint Cream Sauce	1 tablespoon Dijon mustard
1 tablespoon dry vermouth	1 tablespoon scraped onion

Combine the Cream Sauce with the other ingredients and freeze. Reheat in a double boiler. Season with salt and pepper if necessary.

Onion Sauce

Serve with veal, egg, lamb and some vegetable dishes.

1 pint Cream Sauce	4 tablespoons butter or
1 pound (4-5 medium) onions	margarine

Prepare the Cream Sauce and set aside.

Peel and chop the onions by hand or in a food processor.

Cook the onion for 1 minute in rapidly boiling salted water. Drain and press out excess liquid.

Heat the butter in a heavy saucepan and stir in the onions. Reduce the heat to very low and cook covered for 15 minutes. The onions must not brown.

Combine with the Cream Sauce. Cool thoroughly before freezing.

Mushroom Sauce

Serve with egg, fish, shellfish and meat dishes.

1 pint Cream Sauce	2 tablespoons Madeira or
½ pint duxelles or ½	sherry
pint frozen raw	Few drops gravy coloring
mushrooms	

Thaw the sauce. Reheat in a double boiler, adding the duxelles (or frozen mushrooms), wine and coloring. Stir until blended.

If you prefer the frozen raw mushrooms, thaw them enough to separate the pieces and sauté them in 2 tablespoons of butter until all the liquid has disappeared. Then add the mushrooms to the sauce.

Stocks for Soup or Sauces

Anyone seriously interested in cooking will always have a supply of meat, fish and poultry stock on hand. The simplest way is to cook it when convenient and store it in the freezer.

Brown Meat Stock

3 pounds veal bones	2 bay leaves
3 pounds beef bones	6 sprigs parsley
2 tablespoons sugar	12 peppercorns
2 large onions, thickly sliced	1 large clove garlic
2 carrots, cut in large pieces	2 pounds bottom round, cut in cubes
3 stalks celery (with leaves), cut in large pieces	1 gallon water

Preheat the oven to 475 degrees F. Put the bones in a roasting pan and roast ½ hour, stirring with a large spoon occasionally.

Sprinkle the bones with the sugar and add the vegetables. Roast until the sugar and vegetables are brown. The sugar will caramelize and give color to the stock.

Put the contents of the pan in a large stock pot. Add the meat and 1 gallon of water, the bay leaves and parsley tied together, the peppercorns and the garlic (cut in half). Stir and bring slowly to a boil, removing any scum that floats to the surface. Boil over very moderate heat for 4 hours or until the liquid measures about 2½ quarts. Strain and season to taste with salt. Pour into a container and let cool.

Chill in order to let the fat rise to the top. Remove the fat. Pack in ½-pint and pint containers, leaving ½ inch head space. Label and freeze.

Makes 2½ to 3 quarts stock.

Concentrated Meat Essence (Glace de Viande)

Meat Essence, otherwise known as Meat Glaze or Glace de Viande, is that little extra which famous chefs and especially good home cooks keep on hand. A little square of the substance adds flavor, body and richness to special sauces and gravies.

Boil 3 quarts of rich meat or poultry stock until it is thick and syrupy and measures approximately 1¼ cups. Pour into a small aluminum-foil pan. Cool and refrigerate until firm. (It will be like *very* stiff jelly.) Skim off any fat and cut into 1-inch squares. Cover with 2 sheets of aluminum foil and freeze.

Take out squares as needed, filling the empty spots with a little wax paper before returning the remaining essence to the freezer.

Fish Stock

Prepare this in the summertime when fish are plentiful. It will make all the difference in winter chowders and creamed fish dishes.

2 pounds fish bones and heads, free of skin	6 sprigs parsley
1 large onion, chopped coarsely	12 white peppercorns
1 bay leaf	1½ quarts water

Break the bones into pieces.

Put all the ingredients in a kettle. Bring slowly to a boil, removing any scum that comes to the top. Simmer uncovered for 30 minutes.

Pass through a very fine strainer and taste for seasoning, adding a little salt if necessary.

Cool and pour into ½-pint and pint containers, leaving ½ inch of head space. Label and freeze.

Makes 3 pints.

Canning Bouillon

Canning bouillon takes the place of water when canning some vegetables, adding both flavor and some nutrients. It will keep in the refrigerator for at least 10 days. The bouillon is always added boiling hot.

6 cups water	4 stalks celery (with leaves)
1 teaspoon salt	6 sprigs parsley
1 medium-size onion	1 bay leaf
1 or 2 carrots	1 sprig thyme or
1 turnip	⅛ teaspoon powdered thyme

Put the water and salt in a 2-quart saucepan. Peel and slice the onion into the kettle. Wash the carrots very well and slice them into the kettle. Peel the turnip and slice it into the kettle. Wash the celery well and cut into the kettle. Add the parsley, bay leaf and thyme.

Bring the water to a boil. Reduce the heat and partially cover the kettle. Simmer 60 to 90 minutes. The liquid should be reduced to about 4 cups. Strain, cool and store in a covered jar.

Makes 1 quart.

Index